D0209344

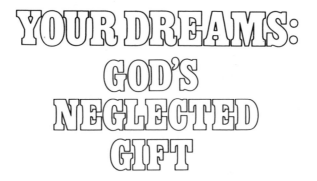

YOUR DREAMS: GOD'S NEGLECTED GIFT

YOUR DREAMS: GOD'S NEGLECTED GIFT

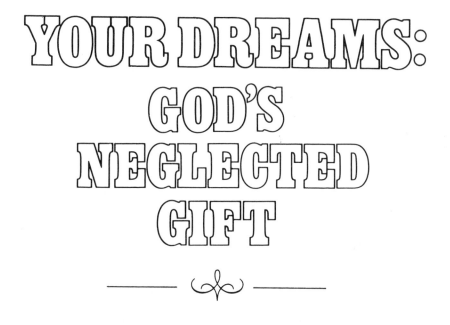

HERMAN RIFFEL

a chosen book

Lincoln, Virginia 22078

All Scriptures are quoted from the *New American Standard Bible,* © The Lockman Foundation, 1960, 1962, 1963, 1968, 1971, unless otherwise identified and are used by permission.

TAB—The Amplified Bible © 1965 by Zondervan Publishing House and are used by permission.

Other Scripture quotations are from *The King James Version of the Holy Bible.*

Library of Congress Cataloging in Publication Data

Riffel, Herman H.
  Your dreams.

  1. Dreams. 2. Riffel, Herman H. I. Title.
BF1078.R48   284.4   81-21635
ISBN 0-912376-77-5   AACR2

YOUR DREAMS: GOD'S NEGLECTED GIFT
Herman Riffel © 1981
Published by
Chosen Books Publishing Company, Ltd.,
Lincoln, Virginia 22078
Printed in the United States of America

*To our dear daughter, Alexis (Elaine),
who is the God-given means of so much
growth and maturing in my life.*

Acknowledgements

I owe my awakening of interest in dreams to God's wonderful working in my life to reveal my inner self to me. He first used Morton Kelsey's lectures to stir my interest. Then He directed me to the Jung Institute, where I came to recognize the validity of the dream and its value. This done, He drove me to the Scriptures, which established in me the importance of the dream's message.

I owe an indebtedness to many who heard my lectures and received help and guidance and thereby persuaded me of the relevance of dreams in this day. Continued help and understanding have come from Lillie, my wife, with whom I have been able to share my dreams and my life for 39 years.

Through the generous offers of George Spaetzel and his family of Kitchener, Ontario, Canada, and Mrs. Marie Martin of Cincinnati, Ohio, we were able to seclude ourselves for long periods of writing in condominiums in Cranberry Village, Collingwood, Ontario, and Hilton Head, South Carolina. Pat Kemp and others offered generous help in typing the manuscript.

It has been a joy to work with my editor, Leonard LeSourd, who persuaded me to write, rewrite, and revise my material until it has come into this form.

I, therefore, pray that through this book others will better understand their dreams and thereby come into a fuller maturity in Christ.

Introduction

When my wife Tib and I drove up to the Florida home of Herman and Lillie Riffel, I was more than a little skeptical. This couple had an unusual ministry—they helped people understand dreams. And that's where the trouble lay.

I'd followed dream interpretation, from a distance, for years. Dreams are a kind of language mirroring the spirit and the soul. But this language is delivered in a secret code which it seemed to me could almost not be learned. Once in a while a genius—like Joseph or Daniel—came along who knew how to unravel the code, but any attempt by ordinary people to do the same seemed mostly futile.

That evening, however, as we sat in the Riffel's living room, I changed my mind.

Tib had been having recurring and troubling dreams. Within an hour, Herman and Lillie helped her understand what her dreams were trying to tell her, not only about the conflicts within herself but about her relation to God.

Their secret?

First, they keep things simple. The Riffels avoid esoteric dream-interpretation jargon. Dreams, they point out, unroll as a series of pictures. Every child understands pictures. Grasping a dream message is a matter of recapturing a skill we once had and—too often—have lost.

Second, they keep things personal. "What does this picture mean to *you?*" Herman asked Tib, noting that even "universal" symbols vary with place and culture.

Third, with the help of dreams, they keep things honest. We so often camouflage our real thoughts and feelings. "Dreams put you in honest touch with what your self has been trying to say *to* yourself," said Herman.

And finally, because truth is now visible, prayer can be more effective. Tib and I have been praying for years about a problem she faced. Now, through her dreams, we could at last pray about the real issue and not just the symptoms.

Dreams, properly understood then, can give us a practical and safe approach to correcting deep-seated problems and to a deeper communion with God.

Since our visit with Herman and Lillie Riffel, we've been asking Him to help us take advantage of our dreams. With them, we feel we have a whole new way of communicating which God has been longing for us to use. We feel that you, too, can find a new adventure through YOUR DREAMS: GOD'S NEGLECTED GIFT.

John Sherrill
Chappaqua, New York

Contents

1

The Dream
That Started It All

It was a beautiful day for mountain climbing. The sky was blue, and the sun had taken off the morning chill. My wife and three children and I had hiked beyond the tree line, well above the hills and forests below.

To the right of the trail, the mountain rose up sharply; to the left, the path dropped off toward the ravine.

I was leading the way, my family right behind me: wife, Lillie, a strong resourceful woman; Elaine, at 19, intelligent and charming; David, 17, with his quick head for mathematics and love of detail; Edward, 13, blue-eyed and blond, our real nature lover.

The trail at the start was about three feet wide and covered with pebbles. It began to narrow as it wound its way up and around the mountainside. Finally the trail was so narrow that we stopped, and I made a sickening discovery. We had come too far; I had led my family into a situation of great peril.

Suddenly I felt the stones give way under my feet, and with a shock, I realized that all of us were going to slide and tumble down into the chasm below!

Then I awoke.

It had been only a dream!

I tried to forget it, but the dream had been too vivid. I could not shake off a feeling that it had some deep significance. But what?

It was the fall of 1964, and Lillie and I were attending a "School for Pastoral Care" conference at a church campground in Grass Lake, Michigan. Only the day before, one of the lecturers had spoken on dreams: "When you have a dream, pay attention to what it says. God may be trying to tell you something."

Next morning the dream of the mountain climb lingered. After lunch I decided to take a walk around the grounds, which were set in beautiful rolling country. They were at the peak of their autumn colors. Migrating geese and ducks were making their landings on the pond below. Finding a quiet spot on the hillside, I sat on the grass to meditate. My spirit was troubled.

Before coming to this conference, I had paid little attention to my dreams, thinking that most of them reflected what I ate before going to bed. Then yesterday's speaker, a distinguished psychologist, author, and clergyman, claimed not only that God speaks to us through dreams, but also that our dreams can warn us about future events.

Now I had to face up to something. Last night's vivid dream was saying something to me. It might be something I didn't want to hear, but I could not dismiss it. If God were trying to get my attention, He had certainly succeeded.

In the dream I had led my family in a direction that had brought us all disaster. Could there be a parallel in real life?

On the surface, the answer was no. I was pastor of a small church in St. Clair Shores, Michigan, dedicated to my flock, a faithful husband and committed father.

But there was a small worm eating at this healthy situation, and I knew it. To most men and women it would seem harmless, this little fantasy world of impure thoughts I was building up in my mind. I had it firmly under control, I told myself, and it had no bearing on my ministry or my family.

"You're making a mountain out of a molehill, Herman," many of my friends would have said if I had shared this with them.

Deep down I knew better. In my study of human nature, I understood perfectly well that almost all the mischief we do in this world begins with a thought. My thought life was off the track, and if I let it develop further, the thought could lead to the misdeed.

As I sat there on the hillside in the midst of autumn splendor, I went through a process I had always advised others to follow when they knew they had done something wrong: confess it to God, repent of it, and believe that God has forgiven you.

I did this.

I also did something else that day which was to affect the rest of my life.

I concluded that my indifferent attitude toward dreams had been wrong. There was something here that demanded my attention. I needed to know more about dream interpretation as a possible tool not only for helping myself, but also other people.

Driving home from the conference, I tried to express some of my thoughts to practical-minded Lillie. She had also been impressed by the freshness of the teaching at the meetings.

"The classes on dreams made the greatest impression on me," I began.

"Yes, with me too." I could feel Lillie's eyes studying me. "Do you think you can use dreams in your counseling?"

"Not yet. But I want to learn how."

"You'll have to be careful, Herman." She was remembering that leaders of our orthodox denomination were already worried about the spirit of renewal sweeping through Protestant churches.

I sighed. "Why are church officials always so threatened by change? Are we afraid we'll lose control? God is supposed to be the Head of the church, not man."

"I know, Herman. We've been over this ground before."

We sure had. How often I had been disturbed by the rigidity of the ecclesiastical system. But for 20 years now I had kept my life and feelings under tight control as I tried to shepherd my small flock. Meanwhile the Spirit of change was moving faster and faster. Deep down, I wanted to be a part of it.

"I'm going to start recording my dreams when we get home," I announced to my wife. Then I reminded her that we had been urged to keep a pencil and pad handy on the table beside our bed to write down our dreams before we forgot them. We were to do this in the middle of the night because we might not remember them by morning.

Lillie was shaking her head. "If we both keep turning the light on and off during the night, neither of us will get any sleep." Lillie was a much lighter sleeper than I.

"Are you going to do it, too?" I asked her, surprised.

"I'm thinking about it."

In the silence that followed, I thought over some of the key statements about dreams that I had heard during the past few days:

The dream is an invaluable counselor. We cannot pay for a better one.

It is with us every night, charges no fee, and makes no demands except that we listen to it and learn to detect God's voice in symbolic language.

The dream seeks to cooperate with His great purpose: to help us realize every part of our potential and to bring us into harmony with ourselves, God, and the world around us.

There is no better way to get to the heart of our problems than through our dreams.

The challenge of these statements intrigued me. I sensed that they threatened change in almost every area of my life.

2

A Shocking Dream

After returning home, the first thing I did was to place a pad and pencil on the table beside my bed for the recording of my dreams. Those that seemed significant were later transferred into a notebook. At first, about one out of every five dreams seemed to have meaning for my life. This percentage was to increase, until today I find that four out of five dreams are pertinent.

Right away, I began having dreams that related to our family situation—particularly to David, our eldest son, who was a freshman at nearby Wayne University. Because of our tight economic circumstances, he was living at home while attending classes. I should have been prepared for a series of confrontations with him when be began a course in philosophy, but I wasn't.

In rapid order, David challenged my traditional Christian beliefs about the divinity of Christ, the Trinity, the Ten Commandments, and a few others I can't recall. We argued. Then David shifted his attack to our way of life. He claimed it was narrow. Old-fashioned. When, he asked, were we going to become a part of the 20th century?

This transformation from the kindness and thoughtfulness he had shown as a teenager to belligerence and condemnation troubled me. David also wanted no restrictions on his new life-style. I could have accepted that if he hadn't been living at home and driving the family car. When I insisted on certain limitations on his coming and

going in connection with the use of our car, the relationship was further strained.

Then I had a dream:

>It was night, and I was alone in the basement of a department store. All the counters were covered over with muslin cloths. Suddenly I saw a policeman break into the store. This was illegal. I went to the telephone and called police headquarters for help. A policewoman came. The policeman and the policewoman faced each other with their guns drawn.
>
>Then the scene changed, and I was on the floor of the living room of our home. My mother was standing on the landing of the stairs leading to the second floor. We had our guns pointed at each other. Then I shot, and she fell.

I awakened with a terrible sense of remorse. How could I have done such a thing? I loved my mother. She was a gentle, loving woman.

Yet the picture in the dream was so vivid it was unforgettable. I was badly shaken. There must be some reason for the dream. But what?

I wondered if it related to an incident that had happened the day before. Our son, who had come from the university in a particularly combative mood, had challenged something I said. We had angry words, and David stalked away to his room, leaving me shaken and white-faced.

Could this horrible dream have anything to do with David? Nothing I understood then about the interpretation of dreams helped me, but the nightmare frightened me so much that I made a special effort to ease the tension between David and myself.

Things went a bit more smoothly after that, but I did not forget the dream. Then Lillie and I spent an evening with Dr. and Mrs. Francis Whiting, two close friends whose knowledge of dream interpretation far surpassed mine. When I told them of the nightmare, they both became very alert.

"Did you notice the two authority figures in the dream?" Dr. Whiting asked.

I had not thought of the policeman and the policewoman in those terms.

"They symbolize some kind of authority within," my friend continued. "It may be the voice of a father or mother, a teacher, the law, the church, or your conscience. We all have voices of authority within us."

"I can see that," I said.

"There are two sets of masculine and feminine figures in your dream," he went on to say. "These speak of the masculine and feminine parts of you which need to be in balance."

I did not really understand this principle, although it had been touched on at the conference. There, it had been tied to the Scripture: "And God created man in His own image, in the image of God He created him; male and female He created them" (Genesis 1:27).

"But why should mother and I be pointing guns at each other?" I asked. "There were never guns in our Mennonite home, except for hunting, and I have never seen one in my mother's hands."

"You and your mother are somehow related to the police officers in the dream. Think about it, and you'll find the application," Francis said.

I did ponder it. If the policeman who broke into the store represented the masculine part of me, then this part of me was out of hand, just like the man who shot his mother. According to Dr. Whiting, these two males were symbols of authority in me. If so, my masculine nature was too hard and unbending.

This was too deep and searching a dream for me to deal with at the time. I sensed that the conflict with my son was only a reflection of another conflict inside me, a conflict of authority which had never been resolved and now had been carried over to my relationship with my son.

The dream came at a time of intense inner struggle, when I was resisting the rigid doctrines of the institutional church on one hand while trying to cope with the rebellion of my children on the other. I knew unconsciously that I had not resolved that inner struggle of which the dream spoke. I did not know which authority to follow. Or to what degree. And the situation between my son and me was so tense that I needed to know.

My dreams were probing into me so deeply that there were times

I wished I had never gotten involved in this area. My dreams were so devastatingly accurate they seemed to be the mirror of my soul—just as accurate and just as unflattering as my reflection in the bathroom mirror when I stared into it upon first awakening in the morning.

Did I want to continue looking at such revealing pictures of my soul? Would it not be much better to forget all about dreams and just let them fade away at the beginning of the day?

Two forces were at war inside me: one stirring me to seek, to explore, to change old established patterns of belief and thinking; the other urging me to play it safe, to be cautious, to look with hard skepticism at these new (to me) concepts.

For weeks I stood at a crossroads, wondering which way to go.

3

The Search Continues

I'm not sure how I made the decision that was so radically to change my life. The seed was planted at the Grass Lake conference. My spirit had been so refreshed there that the old patterns of my life seemed dead. The subject of dreams was only one facet of a transformation that was slowly taking place inside me, urging me to make more of an adventure out of life. I doubt if I could have brushed aside my growing interest in dreams, even if I had wanted to. Then books on dreams appeared, including *Man and His Symbols* by Carl Jung, and I was much impressed with the work being done on this subject at the Jung Institute in Zurich, Switzerland. I was also surprised to discover a growing interest in dreams at a number of universities in the Western world.

From my research in the months that followed, some interesting facts emerged. I learned that each night most people dream at least an hour, during which time there are several dream periods. The sleep pattern seemed to be comparable to the varying depths of water between the shore and the ocean depths. Offshore are the shallows, next the shelf, and then the deep water. Sleep is first in the shallows, next on the shelf where dreaming takes place, then deep sleep.

I learned that there are physical manifestations correlated with dreaming, that doctors can check the brainwaves of the sleeper with an electroencephalograph and determine when a person is dreaming. An even simpler method is to watch the eyes of a sleeper. When he is dreaming, his eyeballs move under the eyelids because the dreamer is literally watching a picture.

Thus the biblical words of Nebuchadnezzar are accurate when he said, "I saw a dream" (Daniel 4:18 author's paraphrase).

Watching a sleeper's eyeballs move back and forth, a friend later asked him, "Were you dreaming of a tennis match?"

"No," said the dreamer, "I was watching my neighbors toss tomatoes back and forth over the fence."

I stored away all the information I could find. The effect of my alarm clock, for example. We had been warned that a loud alarm clock can jar from our memory the details of a dream. My particular clock had a unique pattern. About two or three seconds before the alarm rang, there would be a little "tick" which I suppose would be comparable to the cocking of a gun before firing. The "tick" could barely be heard before the alarm would drive away all sleep.

One morning as I was fast asleep and in the midst of a dream, I heard the "tick," and it found a place in my dream. The dream went on with various scenes before the alarm went off. I wrote down the dream and the sequence of events. Putting it all together, I realized that in the two or three seconds between the "tick" and the alarm, a story was unraveled that took a long time to tell, and much longer to write down. In comparison, an hour's dream must contain volumes of material.

As the weeks passed, I found myself increasingly successful in recalling my dreams. One night I might be running and running and getting nowhere. Or I would try to move but my legs were too heavy. Or I would wander from one building to another, looking for the class I should be attending. I might dream of sliding over a cliff and barely hanging on to an overhanging shrub. I might be falling, and wondering when I was going to land. Or I would be charged by an elephant or a bull and awaken with a hammering heart.

Then again, I might be delightfully flying through the air without the use of a plane. Or proudly giving orders to the President of the United States, or successfully traveling to the moon. Some dreams would be amusing enough to become the subject of table conversation, but some would be so embarrassing I would not tell them to anyone.

Though I could interpret only a few of these dreams, my overall knowledge of the subject was growing. I had learned that dreams are common to all men, in Western, Eastern, or primitive cultures. Everyone dreams, unless prevented by alcohol or drugs.

I was impressed that *if God made every man dream for one hour per night through his lifetime, and only unnatural interference like alcohol and drugs inhibited dreaming, then dreams must be of value.* Obviously, then I should not disregard my dreams.

Yet if dreams were so important, why hadn't the church taught us about them? I had never heard a sermon on dreams. It was true that the dreams of the Bible were occasionally alluded to, but always as side information. "That was how God spoke in the past," a theologian might say, implying that God didn't speak that way anymore. Furthermore, all that was said by my professors about dreams in the years of my training for the ministry could be put into a ten or fifteen-minute capsule. And my training had been biblically oriented and evangelical. We had studied the Bible thoroughly. Why were dreams not included? I went to the Scriptures themselves to seek an answer.

I discovered that references to dreams (that come while we are asleep) and visions (that come while we are awake) were not only in the Old Testament, as I had thought, but they filled the New Testament as well. Once I began to study, I found the references were almost unending. Abraham, Jacob, Joseph, Gideon, and Solomon were led or encouraged by dreams. Joseph and Daniel saved their nations because they were able to interpret dreams correctly. The prophets got their messages through dreams and visions. God said to Moses, "Hear now My words: If there is a prophet among you, I the Lord shall make Myself known to him in a vision. I shall speak with him in a dream." (Numbers 12:6). No wonder I found the frequent references to dreams and visions in the prophetic books.

Major events of the Bible hinged on dreams or visions. When God wanted to give Abraham the great promise concerning his nation, He put him into a deep sleep, and then spoke to him. God wanted to save Israel, so He gave Pharaoh a dream.

I was amazed to see how extensively dreams were used in the New Testament. Joseph had not taken Mary as his wife when he discovered that she was "with child." Then Joseph had a dream in which an angel of the Lord appeared to him, saying, "Joseph, son of David, do not be afraid to take Mary as your wife; for that which has been conceived in her is of the Holy Spirit." (Matthew 1:20).

That Joseph believed and immediately obeyed the message of the dream spoke volumes to me about the confidence that these people had in dreams.

There were visions given to Zacharias and Mary; Moses and Elijah were seen in a vision. Paul received his call in a vision, Peter his commission to go to the Gentiles.

It might seem that after the Holy Spirit came, there would have been no need for dreams and visions. Not so. "And it shall be in the last days, God says, That I will pour forth My Spirit upon all mankind; and your sons and your daughters shall prophesy, and your young men shall see visions, and your old men shall dream dreams" (Acts 2:17).

I found five dreams and three visions surrounding the birth of Christ. At the transfiguration, Jesus was encouraged by a vision. Finally, when God wanted to give great revelations of the future, He did it by giving John visions on Patmos.

Adding together all the direct references to dreams and visions, all the stories surrounding them, and all the prophecies that issued out of them, I discovered that about one third of the Bible is related to dreams and visions.

Why then had the church, especially the evangelical church, overlooked so much valid material, especially when it boasted that its members believed the Bible—all of it? As an evangelical myself, I recognized that we did believe the Bible's record of dreams, that is, that God once spoke to men through dreams and visions. But why did we not believe that God still speaks to man in dreams and visions today? The answer I found came as a shocking revelation from Greek pagan thought, not Judeo-Christian tradition at all.

My research uncovered the fact that many centuries ago, the Eastern world accepted dreams and visions, but the Western world took a negative and unbelieving attitude. Why? We have to go back into history to find the reason not only for our rejection of dreams and visions, but also for our rejection of other supernatural phenomena common to the Scriptures.

Plato taught that there were three valid sources from which man could obtain knowledge. The first was from the five senses—seeing, hearing, smelling, touching, and tasting. Man shared this sensory aptitude with the animal world.

The second source of knowledge, Plato said, was reason. Here we moved beyond the animal world and with our minds came to conclusions beyond our sensory abilities. Naturally, we trained our minds to look at a situation and think out the solution to the problem.

The third valid source of knowledge, according to Plato, was the spiritual realm, which he called "divine madness."

He considered this realm to be just as valid as the others, teaching that just as the body is subject to the mind, so the mind is subject to the spirit.

Then in came Aristotle as Plato's successor. He and his followers ruled out the validity of the spiritual as a third source of knowledge, maintaining that knowledge had to come by the five senses or by reason only. This humanistic philosophy was transmitted throughout the Western world. Since the Western world lived under Aristotelian philosophy for centuries, the Western secular world, and tragically the Western church, were deeply affected.

Lillie and I saw the effects of this rationalistic philosophy in our own church and community, where there was a growing separation between the secular and the spiritual worlds. Many people would go to church on Sunday and then enter the business and professional world on Monday, seeing no connection at all between the two. The members of a church would pray for a person about to have an operation; then the medical team, often without any faith in God, would perform its scientific work. The secular world was built on a science based on mathematics and sensory knowledge; the spiritual world often ignored scientific discoveries; and the two acted as though they did not need each other.

In our later travels we saw how different it was in the Eastern world. The prominent position of temple gods on every street corner and over every important building in East Asian countries gave clear evidence that their business was closely related to their religion. The primitive tribes in the jungles of South America, New Guinea, and Africa also lived in constant contact with the spiritual world, making offerings to the spirits for the success of every venture. During a football game in New Guinea, the contest was stopped as team A accused team B of putting a curse on them. The action was halted so that team B could plan a spiritual counterattack.

All this seems farfetched, even ridiculous to Westerners, but it indicates the oneness between the spiritual and physical worlds in the minds of these people.

Aristotelian philosophy did not allow for dreams and visions, nor prayer, nor spiritual manifestations of God, nor angels, nor Satan and demons. Since Aristotle had so influenced Western thinking, including Christianity, and since dreams and visions are not controlled by the rational mind but come via the unconscious, humanistic-minded Westerners pronounced them either nonsensical or at best unreliable. Yet all of these manifestations were common to the men and women of the Bible. Spiritual manifestations had not changed since that day, but Western man's atitude toward them had changed because he had allowed himself to be limited by a philosophy that could not contain them.

I'll never forget how shocked I was when a pastor friend once showed us his "cutout" Bible. He had taken an ordinary Bible and cut out of it all the portions that the Western church did not accept as relevant for today. Among parts cut out were dreams and visions, as well as the supernatural works of Jesus and the Holy Spirit. He showed us a Bible with pages that had verse after verse cut out, some where only the margin was left. Then he made this significant statement: "The liberal says that miracles can't happen, and the fundamentalist says they won't happen. The practical results are the same."

These disclosures were like a thrust of a sword right into my heart, for members of our denomination always prided themselves on believing the Bible from cover to cover, including the words on the cover that proclaimed, "Holy Bible." My discoveries shook the secure foundations of my Protestant evangelical tradition. We boasted that we had not yielded to the liberal theology that questioned the inspiration of the Scriptures, yet now I was being shown that we had actually ignored great portions of the Word.

I had read through the Bible more than thirty times. It seemed impossible that I should have such a blind spot. Yet none of my reading and study had ever included the study of dreams. My thinking had gone along with the statement in the *International Standard Bible Encyclopedia,* commonly used among Evangelicals at that time: "Dreams are abnormal and sometimes pathological. Sleep is a normal experience. Perfect and natural sleep should be without dreams of any conscious occurrence. . . . The Bible, contrary to a notion perhaps too commonly held, attaches relatively little religious significance to dreams."

As I began to venture outside my early framework of beliefs, I found that I was not being taken outside of scriptural teaching but further into it. As I looked into *Strong's Concordance,* I found 224 direct references to dreams and visions in the Bible.

My study of dreams in Scripture convinced me that I had certainly had a blind spot in my theological eye. If this were true in connection with dreams, what about my attitude toward other portions of the Scriptures? I hated hypocrisy and wanted to be true to my God in all things, especially in my attitude toward His Word.

Had the time come for me to face up to all this?

4

Crisis

As my knowledge of dreams grew, so did my ability to interpret them. One day I had this dream:

Alone in my car I was following a bus down a dirt road, and the bus threw so much dust in the air, I could hardly see where I was driving.

This dream disturbed me for two reasons. I had learned that a bus in one's dream represents the crowd. Furthermore, the dust in the air indicated I was too confused to see where I was going.

When I described the dream and my interpretation to Lillie, she nodded her head. "The Lord seems to be telling you to follow Him instead of the crowd."

Inside, I was in ferment. There was a crisis in my spirit because deep down I knew that my three-hundred-member church in St Clair Shores in the suburbs of Detroit was too greatly influenced by the world about it. Spiritual matters were measured by outward success: How large was the church? How beautiful were its buildings? How well known was its pastor? How lovely was the music? By the early 1960's, this had produced in me a spiritual atrophy; I felt manipulated and controlled by people and by outer circumstances, not by God.

The dream forced me to take action. I began to rethink my beliefs in the light of new discoveries. Along with my growing research on dreams had come a sense of excitement about the movement of the Holy Spirit. As I opened myself to this new freshness, my inner spiritual life was quickened.

God continued to press me harder. Desperate needs were arising in the church. One day I received an urgent call to come to a hospital in downtown Detroit. There I was met by two of my parishioners. In tears, they told me that their seven-year-old son, Kenny, had a rapidly developing brain tumor. The doctors could do nothing more, and their prognosis was that Kenny had just a few more months to live.

"We can take him to a healing service at another church," his mother said, "but if God can do it there, He can do it at our own church."

She put the problem in my lap. In my ministerial training, I had learned a theology that was based on logic. Healing had been put into the hands of doctors. That Jesus had commanded the disciples to heal made good history, but it was not practical for today. But now the question was put before me by the need of one seven-year-old boy. What would I do with it?

It was one of those turning points we all come to at different times in our lives. I knew if I opened myself to the mystery of healing, other mysteries would soon challenge me. All the workings of the Holy Spirit were mysteries, and yet they were all performed through the disciples and the New Testament church.

I struggled hard with all this. If I took a new course, where would I stand with the people to whom I had taught systematic theology for so long? How would my fellow ministers accept me? What reaction would I trigger in the small denomination I had served faithfully for 25 years?

On one side, I saw the cost involved; on the other was that mysterious power which the disciples had and for which I longed to meet the great needs around me. As Lillie and I prayed about all this, we centered on this promise of Jesus: "He who believes in Me, as the Scripture said, from his innermost being shall flow rivers of living water" (John 7:38).

An inner craving began inside me to find the fountain from which the living waters flow.

At the Grass Lake conference, I had watched Dr. Albert Heustis, Health Commissioner for the State of Michigan, lay his hands on the sick and pray for God's healing. He did not reject medicine; he made prayer a partner to it. And so I did the same with little Kenny.

We prayed often for this little boy. Instead of leaving us in two or three months, he lived for four more years. Not only did he live, but he received an inner gift of hope and faith that he shared with his parents, comforting them.

I moved forward in my counseling. In the process I discovered that the deep problems of people were often reflected in their dreams, and that the interpretations often revealed the necessity for changes in their life-styles. When I wasn't sure of an interpretation, I could usually get the help I needed from several specialists in the field.

As I learned more about the Holy Spirit, a new joy and anticipation began to take hold of me. It became evident in my life and preaching. As others were touched, they wanted to hear and learn about these mysteries. All the manifestations of the Spirit soon became evident in our church, even if the evidence was small. I was reminded that life in an acorn is just as real as in an oak tree, and all the potential of the mighty oak is present in the tiny seed.

The results in the lives of people who were open to the Spirit were exciting. Husbands and wives became reconciled; emotional and physical healings resulted. A new Power was being transmitted through me that healed destructive attitudes and behavior patterns.

But just as the mystery of God's supernatural working thrilled and changed those who hungered and thirsted after it, so did it become a threat to those who claimed they already had all that the Christian life offered. For them, the mere suggestion that there could be *more* challenged their security.

Meanwhile changes continued to take place in me, changes that had begun with my receptivity to the movement of the Holy Spirit. Through dream revelations I'd begun to open up my inner life to Christ in a new way. My dreams had begun to show the blind spots which I had never seen, where fear and pride and prejudice could hide. It was as Jesus said, "For from within, out of the heart of men, proceed the evil thoughts and fornications, thefts, murders, adulteries, deeds of coveting and wickedness, as well as deceit, sensuality, envy, slander, pride and foolishness. All these evil things proceed from within and defile the man" (Mark 7:21-23).

I now had an intense desire to be set free from the devouring dragons of the past and take the path that Jesus had described to His followers: "If anyone wishes to come after Me, let him deny himself, and take up his cross daily, and follow Me. For whoever wishes to save his life shall lose it, but whoever loses his life for My sake, he is the one who will save it. For what is a man profited if he gains the whole world, and loses or forfeits himself?" (Luke 9:23-25).

This death and resurrection process spoken of by Jesus was also being pointed to in my dreams, which though painful, had started me toward the first real fulfillment I had ever experienced. For me, the soaring highs of the Spirit, valid as they were, needed the balance that came from dealing with the uncleanness of the inner man.

Soon I began to face sharp questions about "these new doctrines" in the deacons' meetings. I explained that they were not new but old; they were just new to us. I offered my belief that the New Testament was valid for today, just as it stands, including all the mysteries and miracles and visions and dreams. I pressed forward with the full ministry of all that God had for us.

Did I move too fast? Was I stubborn and insensitive to these people? I tried not to be. The confrontation that occurred has been repeated in hundreds, perhaps thousands of churches since then.

I remember the agony of spirit I had when one of my trustees, speaking, he said, for many people in the church, asked me to resign. I told him I would pray about it and give him my answer the following week. That night I broke the news to Lillie.

"Can you think of any good reason to resign?" she asked.

"To protect the peace of the church."

"Jesus wasn't very peaceful when He felt changes should be made."

"But to continue to fight will be painful and costly. Is it right to put the congregation through this?"

"Only if you feel that God wants this congregation to change. If He does, then how you feel about it isn't very important."

As usual, Lillie went to the heart of the matter. I checked it all out with my children, too. They were solidly supportive and urged me to do what I felt was right.

I reported back to the trustees and told them I could not resign from a job to which I felt God had called me. The trustees then set up a congregational meeting for several weeks later to vote on whether I should be permitted to continue my ministry or be dismissed.

The night before the meeting, further evidence came that God uses dreams and visions to speak to us. We had been invited to attend a home prayer meeting in another community some distance away. No one knew Lillie and me except the man who had invited us. He introduced us, but gave no information to the group about our church crisis.

This group had met every Tuesday evening for five years. They knew each other well, met informally, and sought the guidance of the Holy Spirit.

About half an hour into the meeting, a local artist who owned a studio in town had a vision:

I see a beautiful belt that has many fingers proceeding out from it and hairlike projections from the fingers.

Did anyone understand what it meant?

A time of prayer followed, after which a woman received a word of knowledge that this vision concerned Lillie and me. We were not to be bound, even by a belt that was beautiful. We were to be free.

Then the artist spoke again. He said the belt was a Protestant denomination, the fingers were the churches, and the hairlike projections extending from the fingers were people. God would let us be a blessing to many within the belt, but we were not to hold onto it. We were to let go in an attitude of humility.

What a help that vision was the following night! Lillie and I sat through the congregational meeting with not only a feeling of peace, but even some detachment. The vote was close, but against me. I was dismissed as pastor.

We were free, all right! And what could have been the most painful and humiliating experience of our lives had been turned around so that we felt released to move forward to the exciting new life God had promised.

5

The Adventure Begins

Being fired from my job was a painful experience, even though it was tempered by our certainty of the Lord's hand in it. Lillie helped me through the rejection and my tendency to second-guess myself.

"I suppose it was a mistake to go into so many new areas of ministry," I said to her one morning.

"Why, when so many people were helped?"

"Not enough to swing the vote though."

Lillie didn't answer, but I knew she was thinking that my self-pity was showing. I had to air it all before I could get on with life.

"From the moment I introduced these people to renewal, everything seemed to go wrong," I ventured.

Lillie laughed. "You don't know how funny that sounds. They're not children. They need to be renewed, to be alive to all that God has for them."

"Perhaps we moved too quickly on it. Maybe we should have presented it in stages."

"Perhaps." Lillie shrugged. But she knew and I knew that we had not gone overboard with the teachings which were so invigorating to some and repellent to others.

"Herman, it doesn't take much to disturb a church today," she continued. "You could have stayed with the safe conventional doctrines and not ruffled any feathers. But you would have had just another dead church and, in my opinion, been only half the man you are now."

Tears came to my eyes, and I hugged her.

We decided to trust that God was moving us from the Michigan church into a new work. Shortly thereafter I had the following dream:

The waters of a flood were covering much of the City of Detroit. People had left the area. I went to check our house and found it empty.

I had learned that a house in one's dreams speaks not of the physical, but of one's psychological house, that is, the house of the soul. The old psychological house in which I had lived was the church and our denomination, which had provided a measure of security for many years. But now that house was empty, because I had been forced to leave it.

As Lillie and I prayed for direction and read the Bible together, once again I focused on these words of Jesus: "If any man is thirsty, let him come to Me . . . and drink. He who believes in Me. From his innermost being shall flow rivers of living water" (John 7:37,38).

I saw this stream as one that came forth from God; all who yielded themselves to the Spirit of God thus became channels of it. Soon the stream was reflected in my dreams. First it was small so I could step over it, next it became a brook, and then it was a mighty river.

One night I had this dream:

I was pushing a baby carriage with a little baby in it. When I came to the end of the street, I did not stop but pushed the carriage right up over a two-story house. The house was like the one we were living in at the time. Once I even lifted the carriage over my head, and the baby fell out, but I caught it.

I had trouble interpreting this dream. It seemed ridiculous that I did not push the carriage around the house, but went over it instead. My friend Francis Whiting pointed out to me that the dead end of the steet represented the "dead end" of my ministry in St.

Clair Shores. But I was not to stop. Instead, I was to carry the baby (new idea or concept) right up over the top of the traditional house in which my soul was then living. Though I might have to lift the carriage over my head to get there, and the baby might even fall out, yet I would not lose it (the new idea).

This was an important dream because it showed me once again that God was guiding my life—and that one of the ways He was speaking to me was through my dreams. But dreams were not the only way or the most important. What God said to me through Scripture and in answer to direct prayer were still my primary avenues for receiving His guidance.

Though Lillie and I had become increasingly aware of how valuable dreams were in hearing the voice of God, we were frustrated by our limited knowledge of how to interpret dreams, as well as by skepticism of many Christian friends. I wanted to go directly to a school for some training in dream psychology, but our finances were too limited for me to stop working. Since two of our children were still in school and needed our support, I accepted a position as chaplain on the staff of Radio Station HCJB, the World Radio Missionary Fellowship in Quito, Ecuador.

During the next year, as new opportunities opened for teaching and counseling in Ecuador, my inner yearning to know more about dreams and their interpretation, in order to help people live more effectively, began to diminish. Then one night I had this dream:

> *I was on a raft some distance from the shore where people were swimming. The water was deep. A young girl was in my care. Suddenly she fell off the raft and sank headfirst into the deep water. I quickly dived after her, grabbed her by the heel, and pulled her out of the water and onto the raft.*

I awakened badly shaken, for in the dream I knew I was responsible for the girl's safety and care. When the interpretation came, I realized the girl in this dream was the baby I had pushed in the carriage, grown older now. I had been neglecting her (that new truth) and she had almost been lost, represented by her nearly drowning in the deep water.

I needed to pay attention to that truth again, care for it, nurse it into full maturity. My thoughts turned to the Jung Institute in Switzerland where I could receive more training. By now our three children were independently making their way in the world. One night I brought up the subject again to Lillie.

"Herman, you've spent 25 years in the ministry. What will psychology training add to your life now?"

Carefully I measured out my answer. "Theology is the systematic study of God. Psychology is the study of man's soul. Each can be lost without the other. If I know more about the deep needs of man's psyche, I'll be better able to apply God's Word and truth to meet those needs."

"I think you're already doing a good job helping people."

"But some problems are so complex, Lillie, I need more knowledge, more discernment, more wisdom."

"But why go all the way to Switzerland?"

"Because I know that the Jung staff, at least most of them, believe in God and the Supernatural. That's not true at many other similar institutions."

Lillie was still not convinced. Agnes Sanford, whose healing ministry we greatly respected, had once said that certain Christians had lost their way while attending classes at the Jung Institute. Lillie called this to my attention.

I pondered it for a long minute. "Those people who lost their way at the Jung Institute might never have really found their way beforehand," I concluded.

Lillie, who can be disconcerting and tenacious in her questions, knows when to slack off. "Since there is no money for such a trip, I guess we can look to the Lord for the answer here," she said. "If He provides the means for you to go, I will accept that as His confirmation of the whole venture."

"Let's pray that He provides for both of us to go, dear, I have no intention of going there by myself."

Lillie looked surprised, then shook her head. "That's *really* asking for a miracle."

The miracle came about in stages. First, a scholarship was given me to go to Switzerland for my studies. Then a missionary friend in Chile provided a beautiful efficiency studio apartment for us in Zurich at a very reasonable rent. Several other gifts provided the funds needed for Lillie to go with me.

With growing excitement, I sent in my application for admission to the Institute. In it, I outlined the development of my Christian faith, and asked how my experiences fitted into the Institute's psychological framework. Weeks later, a reply came back, accepting me as a student. Later I learned that they considered my experiences not only valid, but a natural step in the development of Christian maturity.

We arrived in Zurich in April. Within weeks the city was ablaze with spring colors: beautiful flowers, shrubs, neatly manicured yards, and flowering trees with wisteria hugging the varying types of architecture. We rented a studio room at the Mission Catholique Francaise, a place where priests would normally stay for periods of study. It had a kitchenette behind an accordion screen, a trundle bed, table, bookshelves, clothes closet, and two chairs. And it was only a short walking distance from the Institute.

At the Institute, courses were taught in English during the day and in German at night. Since we spoke both languages, we selected courses from both day and evening sessions. This was helpful because we needed to increase our German vocabulary, which had been limited to a combination of household and religious expressions in our homes and churches. Now we would be learning psychological terms in the German language, too.

Though Dr. Jung had died several years before I enrolled in his Institute, Lillie and I had seen several excellent films on his life, had read his books, and felt we knew him and his work well. Then one night shortly after our arrival, I had this dream:

Dr. Jung was still alive, and I was traveling with him in the United States. He and I got into his car, which was built with

three tandem wheels about ten feet apart. I knew he would
have trouble with his car on the road since it was so long and
unwieldy, though it looked expensively made. He drove onto
the road and was soon stopped by a policeman who asked
him if he had paid his taxes. Dr. Jung seemed confused by the
question and said, "I must have." I knew that he would have
further difficulty when I saw that his car had no lights. Then I
awakened.

The dream was not hard to understand. The vehicle Dr. Jung
was driving represented his analytical psychology. The policeman
in the dream was an authority side of me that was questioning Dr.
Jung's views. From the beginning, I knew that his psychology had
no light; psychology, being the study of the soul, has no light in itself. The light has to be provided by God, speaking to man's spirit
by His Holy Spirit.

Lillie and I discussed this dream at length and agreed that it was
given me by the Lord as a warning. We were to allow Christ to be
our light to lead us through the vast corridors of psychological
knowledge. We were to trust in the Holy Spirit to discern what was
good and apply it to our understanding.

Some Christians questioned us later as to why we didn't interpret
this dream as a sign from God that we were to cancel our studies
and return to our homeland. We considered this; in fact, we prayed
for a further word from the Lord about it, and He led us to the
story of Daniel in the Old Testament.

When taken captive from his land, Daniel remained faithful to
his God, who had given him an extraordinary knowledge of
dreams and the ability to interpret them. Recognized by King
Nebuchadnezzar's officials for his intelligence, Daniel was ordered
to study all the literature and language of the Chaldeans. Despite
the fact that the Chaldean religion was without the knowledge of
the true God, and was filled with astrology and occult practices,
Daniel obeyed his captors. He not only studied these things, but
"God gave . . . (him) knowledge and intelligence in every branch of
(their) literature and wisdom . . . ." (Daniel 1:17, words in paren-
theses are mine.)

Later Daniel was able to use his knowledge and gift of dream interpretation in remarkable ways for the glory of God.

My dream and the Scripture to which it led me strengthened my faith that Lillie and I were headed in the right direction, and that God would give us His wisdom through non-Christians as well as believers. I also concluded that since so many branches of the church had ignored, even rejected, dreams and visions and thus lost the understanding of them, it was necessary for some of us to go into the vast and confusing field of dream psychology to find whatever truth there was in it. After all prospective doctors who are also Christians study at secular medical schools to gain basic medical knowledge. Then they ask God for wisdom as to how to use that knowledge for His glory and the benefit of man.

Lillie and I agreed that we needed to find the truth wherever it was hidden, to ask God to enable us to discern the real truth, and to give us the wisdom to use it properly.

6

Back to Basics

Both Lillie and I enrolled for classes which covered the basic principles of analytical psychology. This meant we had to be willing to undergo analysis ourselves.

This would be difficult for both of us, especially for Lillie, who had always been a very private person. We would have to go back into our past and look at some painful experiences and how they had shaped us.

I chose to work with a woman by the name of Dr. Liliane Frey who had been with Dr. Jung for 26 years and had developed rare sensitivity and understanding. During one of our first sessions together, she asked me to describe my childhood years.

I told her I had been born in Canada of Mennonite heritage. My parents, who were from Kansas originally, had tried homesteading in Canada, but the bleak prairies of Saskatchewan made living very difficult. We ended up on a small farm in California.

My parents' lives were centered around the church. When at first we could find no Mennonite church in the Sacramento Valley, our home became the church. The living room was the sanctuary, the bedrooms and porch served as classrooms, and the table was the pulpit for my father's lay ministry preaching. Seldom did a Sunday go by without our attending a church service, first in the home, then later in the little white church building the Mennonite farmers erected for their worship.

We lived in a large farm house, a close-knit family living a very sheltered, simple life. Mother constantly stressed to me the importance of being a good boy. Father read the Bible at breakfast, and in the evening he gathered us for family prayers. Father prayed first, then Mother, and then the children, beginning with the oldest. I was the youngest of nine, and sometimes I would be asleep when my turn came.

During one of our sessions, my analyst drew out of me an experience I had in high school in the little town of Chico, California. It happened on the last day of school, a happy day because it meant that summer work and pay would soon begin in the fruit orchards and gardens.

One day I had been sitting at my school desk when the teacher asked each one in the class to tell something about his plans or hopes for the future. Suddenly one girl did a rather extraordinary thing. Petite, with pretty blue eyes and soft brown locks of hair swishing just above her shoulders, she told us she was going to identify each one of us by a color. An art student, she went on to describe the students in bright oranges, pinks, yellows, reds, and other shades, explaining how the various colors reflected their personalities. When she came to me, she paused a moment, her pretty brow furrowed in concentration.

"I see Herman as black," she said.

I must have looked pained, because she quickly clarified her statement. "I don't mean it in a negative sense. My vision of Herman is black because he is mysterious; much of what he is inside has not been revealed to me."

Dr. Frey was quite interested in this story. "What do *you* think the black represented?" she asked me.

"This young girl had picked up some deception in me," I said reluctantly. "Embarrassed by my background of strict religious training and discipline, I had tried to pull away from it and be someone different."

"What type of person did you want to be with your fellow students?" she pressed.

"Daring and adventurous," I replied after some thought. "But I didn't succeed at this and thus came through as a phony."

"Do you think this young artist would still color you black?" the analyst asked.

I shook my head. "I think I've gone to the other extreme. As pastor of my last church, I was too daring and innovative." Then I told her how the congregation had dismissed me for teaching what they felt were revolutionary new ideas.

Shortly thereafter I had this dream:

In a woods, I came across a deserted castle with a moat around it. I crossed the moat and entered the castle, which seemed to belong to me. A big stream, filled with logs and roots of trees and debris, flowed in front of the castle. The water was swift and came boiling through all the debris. Then I saw a big Canada goose in the water upstream from all the logs. The goose floated down the stream and then went under the logs, coming up on the other side. As it came up, its head and long neck came through a hole in a log, but it could not pull its body through. Becoming tired, the goose fell back into the water, and I did not see it come up again.

When I told her this dream, my analyst became intensely interested. "The castle you discovered is your holy place. That you came upon it and entered it alone is significant. This means you have come into your own as far as your religious life is concerned. The dismissal by your congregation was good for you. It released you from a bondage in which you had surrendered your rights and responsibilities in order to please others."

Dr. Frey went on to say that my crossing the moat surrounding the castle was also significant. Such a moat symbolizes motherly containment. Thus I had also broken strong and perhaps too dependent ties to my mother, freeing me to be more masculine and aggressive.

"What about the stream filled with logs and debris flowing in front of the castle?" I asked.

The river in this case, I was told, was the river of life; the logs were the obstacles to be faced. As wood is often a soft material, here again was softness in my approach to others, the desire to please others above all else. Those obstacles had to be removed so the stream could flow freely.

The final symbol in the dream was the big Canada goose in the water. My analyst suggested it was a good symbol, representing a spiritual attitude. Since I was born in Canada, the goose also represented my Canadian heritage. But the goose, too, was having to struggle against the obstacles in my life that had hampered my spiritual growth: lack of aggressiveness, and the desire to please others. The good news was that this long-established pattern in me was being washed away by the river of life, which also represented the power of the Holy Spirit at work.

"An important point to remember about dream interpretation," stressed Dr. Frey, "is that I could have done nothing with your dream if you hadn't given me the background material about your childhood and church experiences. All dream interpretation has to come from the dreamer. That's why we never attempt quick interpretations requested of us in letters or over the telephone."

It was necessary for me to give my analyst a picture of Lillie, whom I described as cautious in making decisions, suspicious of excessive emotion, but very capable. It had taken one of my rare bursts of aggressiveness to win her.

I had become very lonely while serving as a young pastor in the mining town of Holden, Washington, in the beautiful Cascade mountain range. One day I asked God for a wife, and the thought came that I should look in my school yearbook. I did so and was stopped by a picture of Lillie Hoover. I remembered her as an excellent student and mature person from Detroit, Michigan.

Was this really a sign from the Lord? To make sure, I asked Him to see that she attended our class reunion coming up soon in Portland, Oregan, but I did not communicate with Lillie in any way.

Meanwhile Lillie, again in Detroit, had an urge to go to our class reunion, but we almost didn't make connections. The reunion, in May, 1941, opened with a buffet dinner on a Friday evening at six o'clock. Eight o'clock came, and no Lillie. I decided to wait until nine and then look for someone else. At nine o'clock she walked in!

I was amazed at how totally right she was for me. There was her quiet strength and assurance, her quick mind, the direct way she looked at me, the warmth of her voice and personality, the soft smiles and humor lines that appeared and reappeared on her face. But none of that diminished her femininity.

Convinced that the Lord had brought us together, I made a date to visit her the following week at the ranch of one of her relatives in Granger, Washington. Unfortunately, there was a foul-up in communication, and my bus arrived in Granger after midnight. The streets were deserted, so I started walking.

The only information I had about the location of the ranch was that it was two miles outside of town. But in which direction?

The Lord seemed to point down a particular road, and a two-mile hike brought me to a farmhouse that resembled the one Lillie had described. The name on the mailbox confirmed that I was at the right place, but the house was completely dark. How awkward to wake everyone at such an hour!

I was almost tempted to keep on walking, but I saw a hayfield next to the farmhouse, so I made myself a makeshift bed, lay down, and quickly fell asleep.

The next morning, when I knocked on the farmhouse door, Lillie greeted me as an intrepid explorer who had gone through great hardships to be with her. I proposed to her soon afterward. Cautiously, she held off her decision for a month, but we were married the following October.

Through the first 25 years of our marriage, Lillie had been an anchor point for me, but the tumultuous tempo of recent events had put a great strain upon her. She wanted to be obedient to God, but her steady, cautious nature tended to resist change.

The thought of working with an analyst was discomforting to her, but she agreed to analysis by Dr. Peter Walder, because he had a special understanding and appreciation of Christian symbols, as well as psychological principles. She decided, however, to look him over very carefully in her first appointment and to discontinue sessions if no trust developed between them.

The night before her first appointment, she had a dream which she carefully wrote down and shared with me the next morning:

> *I had just returned home from shopping, carrying packages in my arms. Soon after coming through the front door I noticed my bedroom door was slightly ajar. To my utter surprise, an elderly man was lying in my bed, very leisurely, with his legs crossed so his feet obstructed his view of me. My first thought was, "How dare this man invade the privacy of my room!"*
>
> *The dream scene shifted. Our son David was bringing down from the attic a variety of boxes containing very valuable crystal glasses. I said to him, "Please be very careful as you come down so you do not drop the box and break the crystal."*

At her first analysis session, Dr. Walder explained that he was the elderly man invading her privacy in the bedroom of her dream. The second part of the dream meant that many things of great value were still wrapped up and stored in her unconscious. If she cooperated with the helpful part of herself, represented in the dream by our son David, these treasures could be brought out of the attic of the unconscious memory into conscious life.

Lillie found that interpretation a good beginning, and soon we were sharing our dreams and classroom experiences together in a most creative way.

7

Why Dreams Are Important

As Lillie and I began our courses at the Jung Institute, the immediate writing down of our dreams became essential. Having notebook and pencil handy by the bed was just as important as having them in the classroom since often the seemingly small detail of a dream turns out to be very crucial to the full interpretation.

For example, a small detail in Nebuchadnezzar's dream about the tree that was to be cut down turned out to be very significant (Daniel 4:23). The tree represented Nebuchadnezzar on his throne. That it was to be cut down indicated he would be overthrown. But the seemingly small detail, that *the stump and the roots were to be left*, meant the tree could grow again. And this implied that the king could eventually regain his throne.

"How do I know how important each dream is?" I often asked myself at the beginning of my studies at the Institute.

I soon learned that I could not determine this until the dream was interpreted, and it is hard to interpret a dream without the full picture. Upon awakening at night after a dream, I often resisted writing it down, thinking it was meaningless. I have since discovered that my judgments are often mistaken and can be costly.

The little dream is not little in importance was a principle thoroughly drilled into me. For example, some years after my training in Switzerland, a man coming to me for counseling told me he had seen two little pictures in his dreams. They were such short dreams, he doubted that they had any significance.

In the first, he saw his left leg badly inflamed and swollen, with red veins like dark lines running down it. In the second picture, he saw a very poisonous spider sitting on his brief-case.

To draw out the meaning of the dreams, I asked him for what purpose he used his leg. He said, "To walk, of course."

Then I asked, "Is there something wrong with your 'walk'—your behavior or manner of living?" He was shocked and later admitted that he had a messy situation in his life, but thought he had kept it hidden.

Then I asked what the briefcase represented to him. He said, "My profession," whereupon I suggested that even his work would be affected by his behavior.

The interpretation of these two pictues shocked the man into discontinuing his wrongdoing. Before the dream, he had rationalized that his behavior was "not that bad."

I have learned that there are three particular reasons why we fail to remember dreams.

The first is that we have been taught culturally that the dream is unimportant or irrelevant, and so we have trained our minds not to remember it. Yet if one's attention is called to his dreams, he will usually begin to remember them.

A man once told me he had never had a dream. "I predict that you will remember a dream fairly soon now," I said. Before the week was up, he came, rather embarrassed, to tell me that he had had a dream and wanted me to interpret it.

The second reason we don't remember dreams may be mechanical. The alarm clock, especially the radio alarm, is a great destroyer of dream memory. The dream comes while our mind is still. If, upon awakening, our mind is jarred by an alarm, or by the voice of a radio announcer, the dream is usually lost. For physical reasons as well as spiritual, it is best to awaken quietly and listen to the inner voice of the dream before plunging into the world of the rational mind. If one must have an alarm, then he needs to make notes about his dreams during the night.

The third reason for failure to remember a dream is spiritual. If a person wants to keep God out of his thoughts, he may do so by keeping his mind occupied with other things. So also, a person who does not want to hear the guidance of God through his dreams may be able to shut them out of his memory for a time, but then they will break through in nightmares. On the other hand, the person who respects his deep spirit will want to hear from God. He will give this message to his unconscious, will remember his dreams, and will be helped by them.

Perhaps the main question I asked myself was why the dream is usually so hard to understand. I discovered there are two reasons for this:

First, the dream speaks in a language of symbols that we have to learn to understand, just as we have to learn to understand a foreign tongue (see chapters 8 and 9).

The second and less obvious reason why the dream is hard to understand is that it often shows us our blind spots, those things about ourselves that we do not see, though others may see them in us. When the dream shows our weaknesses by symbols and pictures, we cannot understand what the dream is saying if we have been blind to those weaknesses.

Another question people often ask is, "Why do I dream the same dream over and over?"

The answer: God may be trying to tell you something. If you listen and heed its message, the dream will not repeat itself. I must remember that my dream will change if I change, but it will repeat itself if I persist in my wrong behavior.

Sometimes we will have two or three different dreams the same night, saying the same thing. Pharaoh had a two-part dream in which he first saw seven fat cows being devoured by seven thin ones; next he saw seven full ears of grain swallowed up by seven thin ones (Genesis 41). In his dream, the seven fat cows and the seven full ears of grain represented seven good years. The seven lean cows and the seven lean ears of grain represented seven lean years. Joseph told Pharaoh that his two-part dream was especially significant in that it was foretelling events to come.

Similarly, the two little dreams of the swollen leg and the poisonous spider on the briefcase were saying the same thing in different ways. The swollen leg spoke of the dreamer's inner condition. The spider on the briefcase foretold what would happen if the man continued his wrong behavior.

The basic message of the dream is often twofold, showing the dreamer's present inner condition and then showing what will happen if he continues to go in the direction he is headed. I was amazed to learn these dream principles from my psychological studies and then later to find that these same principles had long ago been put into the Scriptures.

Not every dream, of course, shows both our present inner condition and what will happen in the future. A single dream may have one message. Successive dreams can tell a story, as in a movie. All dreams do not have equal significance; some may defy interpretation even by the experts.

From all of this, it can be seen that *the dream is very personal.* If our work and interests are of national and even international scope, like Daniel's in the Bible, then our dreams will reflect it. If our interests are no larger than our backyard, our dreams are likely to have the same limits.

As Lillie and I studied, it became more and more evident to us that dreams have nothing to do with what we eat before we go to bed. The only connection between dreams and digestion is that the dreamer might be so restless from a full stomach that he will awaken often and thus better remember his dreams. Other points we learned:

The dream is really an inner mind at work. Dr. Austin Hale, of the University of Kathmandu of Nepal, said that when he was a student in college, he would study his math problems intently before going to sleep. Often he would receive the answers to his math problems in his dream. As a linguist in Nepal, he did the same thing, studying the language at bedtime and then receiving many answers to linguistic problems in a dream. The dream can be a valuable computer in a man's unconscious realm.

The kind of attitude we show toward the dream is the kind of response we will receive from it. The dream is like a friend. Treat it well, and a friendship will flourish and bring great returns. Act indifferently toward it, and the relationship will not grow. If we will listen carefully to our dream, write it down, take time to listen to it, follow its instruction, and include it in our journal, it will become a friend and counselor.

8

The Animal in Us

An area of growing interest to Lillie and me has been the role animals played in our dreams. Our teachers pointed out that the whole gamut of emotions—fear, hatred, jealousy, lust, pride, ambition, and anger—come out as animals in dreams.

One night I dreamed that a rhinoceros came charging at me. Frantic with fear, I lunged to one side, and the huge beast went thundering past me. Next I began running in the opposite direction, even though I was close to a herd of elephants. To my surprise, the elephants scattered as I approached them. Then I awoke, breathing hard from fright.

When I reported this dream to my analyst, she reflected a moment. "We've talked before about the difficulty you sometimes have with being aggressive."

"That's right. There have been times when I should have exercised leadership, but didn't."

Dr. Frey reflected a moment. "In a previous session, you mentioned your mother and her influence on your life. Tell me more about her and your father and their relationship to you."

"They were very religious. Father was strict, hard-working, impulsive. Mother was kind and almost saintly. My older brothers worked with Dad on the farm. I helped Mother in the house and was primarily under her influence."

"How did she react to aggressiveness?"

"Her teaching was that we children should be nice and not hurt anyone."

"How did that philosophy affect you?"

I pondered that for a moment. "It kept me from expressing my emotions. In fact, I suppressed my aggressive feelings so much that I developed a temper that would erupt like a volcano."

"What was your mother's response to that?"

"Punishment came from both my mother and father. I learned to keep my temper bottled up, except with my brothers. Yet I knew that was wrong, too, so I tried to suppress my anger even more."

"What happened then?"

Again I groped for the truth—and it came. "The struggle to suppress my anger turned into a strong desire to please people. If I pleased them, I concluded that people wouldn't do things to make me angry. So whenever I was asked a question, the first thought I had was 'What does this person want to hear?' Then I would give the answer I felt would please that person."

"What has been the result of this?"

This interview was getting more and more painful, but I had to meet the issue. "The result was that I began lying to people," I admitted.

"How did your parents handle your lying?"

"They used Scripture to show me how wrong it was. I felt guilty about it and tried to stop it. And did to a large degree. But even as an adult, whenever I was asked a question, the first response from my unconscious would still be, 'What does he want to hear?'"

"Where do you think you are today with these problems? " came the persistent probing.

"Both the anger and lying are under firm control, but my aggressiveness has not found its proper role when confronted by a very aggressive person."

"The rhinoceros in your dream, Herman, is that aggressive part of you. It is chasing you because it wants you to accept it. When animals chase us in our dreams and we turn and face them, they become friendly. We can accept them."

"What shall I do about my anger?"

"When your repressed aggressiveness wants to express itself in anger, let it come out. Don't let it become destructive, but the release of inner aggression can help you assume your proper leadership role. You are fortunate to be studying here with your wife. Ask her to help you let it all come out."

"You mean deliberately let my temper explode with Lillie?"

"Yes."

"She won't like it."

"I'm sure she won't, but she'll want you freed from the restrictions by which you've been bound."

I told Lillie of my conversation with the analyst, and she began nodding vigorously as I described the analyst's reaction to my dream.

"We all want you to be free," she said. "Just try to let your anger come out constructively."

I sat there silently, letting the truth sink in. All these years I had tried to keep my anger under control and to be truthful and kind. Now I was to let it explode so that the hidden energy could be expressed and then properly guided.

"Dr. Frey wants me to let go every time I get angry. She says it will be a kind of home therapy."

I could see Lillie wince, but she didn't resist. "How am I supposed to act?"

"I guess you're just supposed to let me blow off steam."

"Then what?"

"Then we'll talk through whatever it is that made me angry."

She looked doubtful, and I felt silly. Here I was, a middle-aged man, pastor, teacher, counselor—a man who should have accumulated wisdom and maturity—being told to act like a little boy the next time I got mad. Should I stomp my feet? Have a tantrum on the floor? Kick a hole in the door? I knew better than that, but it would be interesting to see what would happen.

The problem was not resolved quickly. I found it hard to let myself go after so many years of "stuffing" things deep inside myself. When I felt an explosion coming, I was self-conscious at first in letting my ire spew out. But the inner bonds did loosen as Lillie and I talked through the subject. The large animals became smaller in my dreams, but other animals continued to appear.

One night I dreamed of a snake.

The next morning in my meditations I asked the Lord what I should do about it. The thought came that Moses had a shepherd's rod which became a serpent when he threw it on the ground. He ran from it, until God commanded him to pick it up by the tail and thus be its master. When Moses obeyed, the snake became a rod of power for him. The word to me was clear. I was not to let a snake or any animal frighten me.

The animal in our dream is not our enemy, even though he looks that way. He is a part of our own energy that has gone wild and needs to become controlled power in our hands. He may also be creative energy that needs to be encouraged, or released. I learned to look carefully at each of the animals in my dreams to see what he was saying to me about myself.

While the snake can be a symbol of wisdom, it is probably a subtle kind of wisdom, as it was in the Garden of Eden. It is not by chance that the fox comes into our dream; our emotional energy is often characterized by the cunning of a fox. Daniel dreamed of the lion and the bear and the eagle, and then of a dreadful beast, all accurately describing various nations of that day. John's visions in the Book of Revelation picture Satan as a dragon who devours, and Jesus as a Lamb Who gives His life, and then rides upon a conquering horse. The horse often speaks of our libido energy.

The great animals—like the rhinoceros, elephant, or bull—can charge and run over us unless we take control. Yet just as God has given man control and dominion over all creatures of the earth (Genesis 1:26, 28), He also gives us control over our emotions if we recognize them and do not deny they are a part of us.

I dreamed I was in a building where there were lions and

tigers. They seemed to be saying to me that they were not dangerous, but I knew they were. The scene shifted, and I was standing beside several children as the animals approached us. Someone seemed to be telling me, "If you have faith, they can't hurt you." So I began to say, "I believe, I believe." And the animals did not touch us.

It is almost lifesaving to some people to know that if we face our fears, they will become our friends. Facing our fears can be done by literally confronting the animal of our dreams upon awakening and asking, "Who are you?" What we are doing is addressing a part of ourselves. The answer may surprise us. When we recognize and accept it, the animal will become friendly in our dreams.

I learned that if I dealt properly with the huge animals that charged me, they would soon leave. Then I had to deal with the cat family, which attacks from behind.

I dreamed I was in a cave-shaped room teaching a young bird to fly. I had a string attached to the bird, and it flew a little. But each time it did, a cat lurking nearby in a pool of water would spring at the bird.

This dream spoke of what was going on in my life. The bird represented the new spiritual part of me I was trying to get airborne. The old emotional nature was represented by the cat in my unconscious (the under water part of me). If not controlled the cat would destroy this new expression of life.

Animals in our dreams accurately portray our emotions or desires, or perhaps our creative expressions. I have taken note of bulls, cows, pigs, bats, badgers, coyotes, mice, rats, frogs, bears, dogs, lions, tigers, ocelots, cats, rams, snakes, spiders, elephants, rhinoceroses, monkeys, turtles, and even prehistoric monsters in my dreams. Each has its own meaning, taken from its own characteristics and its meaning to me personally as the dreamer.

I dreamed I was in an old bedroom which had baseboards

*about six inches high at the bottom of the walls. A whole
stream of rats was running on top of one of the baseboards so
that it was filled with rats from end to end. The rats were
gray, filthy, and diseased.*

This was a sobering dream, because it meant that a stream of evil
thoughts had found an entrance at the lower levels of my life. I confronted these rats, chased them out of the room (my life), and asked
God to do a cleansing and purifying work inside me.

Birds often appear in our dreams. Since they fly in the air, they
may represent our thoughts, our ideas, or even spiritual beings. We
may dream of the dove as a symbol of purity, peace, and the Holy
Spirit, or of the vulture, which feeds upon dead carcasses.

*I dreamed once that Lillie and I were taking a trip in an
automobile. Deciding we would take time to drive into the
mountains on the way to our destination, we climbed up and
up until the road became very narrow. Below us on the right
we saw a green river. Then, in the dusk, a white speck appeared ahead of us and above the end of the road. I saw that
the white speck was the breast of a small eagle sitting in a tree.
When I approached it, the eagle jumped into my arms, and
we wound our way back down the mountain to our
destination.*

At the time I had that dream, we were on a teaching mission to a
group of missionaries. In my journal the next morning I wrote,
"This dream suggests that our visiting this mission is like ascending
to a spiritual height above the river of life. The eagle reminds me of
Isaiah 40:31: 'They that wait upon the Lord shall renew their
strength; they shall mount up with wings as eagles; they shall run,
and not be weary; and they shall walk, and not faint' (KJV)."

The Lord fulfilled that Scripture as He brought great blessing to
many of the missionaries at the conference and provided us with
energy and wisdom during the whole week of seminars and lectures.

The fish in the water can also invade our dreams with a message for us.

I dreamed once that I was catching a really huge trout while on a trip with a friend. Told that I could spear the fish, I said, "No. I have no license to fish here."

This spoke to me about my growing ministry to many small groups, some of which were not officially sponsored by a church, but had approached me privately. I knew that I was given a ministry to speak to such groups, but the dream told me I was to use caution, not aggressiveness (the spear), in the invitations I accepted. I was not to go to churches without official authorization.

As our training continued, Lillie and I became more and more able to help each other with our dream interpretations and with our emotions. One incident is still vivid in my memory. It was about money, always a tinderbox area for men.

My generosity had been questioned. I felt the anger rising, started to check it, then realized I was to let it show. And so I did. I threw the papers in my hand on the floor, exploded at Lillie with a burst of jumbled words and sentences (there's no coherence in an angry outburst), then strode out of the room, banging the door behind me.

It was a good explosion all the way. Unfortunately, the door had a glass pane in it. The glass shattered. Figuring my time and the cost of materials to replace the glass, my therapeutic experience cost me a hundred dollars.

9

The Symbols in Dreams

In Europe, road signs are given symbols. The reason: the people speak different languages, but they can all understand the same picture.

The language of symbols is also the language of dreams and visions. As children, we understand this language of pictures, for it is part of our first learning experiences. As we grow up, we learn to speak in abstract terms, the language of the mind. Unfortunately, many of us have gone too far in the abstract direction; as a result, we are having to re-learn to think in symbolic terms. Without a knowledge of dream symbols and their significance, there can be no proper understanding of our dreams.

"Well, give me a dictionary of terms," you say. "Let's work out a glossary of symbols and their meanings for proper dream interpretation."

That's what I wanted when I first went to the Institute. I thought that if I could find Dr. Jung's list of definitions, I would have the best key to the understanding of dreams. But I never did find such a glossary, and for a very good reason. *There is no single interpretation of any symbol that would hold true for every dream.* A list of dream symbols in which a bicycle means only one thing, and a car means another, would actually be a barrier to the understanding of dreams. This can be shown again and again both from present-day dreams and from the Scriptures.

In Nebuchadnezzar's first dream (Daniel 2), Daniel says that the king is the head of gold. In his next dream (Daniel 4), Daniel's interpretation says the king is the tree that reached up into the heavens. The king was represented by two very different symbols.

The reason there are innumerable symbols in dreams and innumerable meanings of them is that the meaning of the symbol in each dream is drawn from the dreamer and from the message to be conveyed by the dream. With billions of dreamers, and multiplied billions of messages, it is best to give up the search for a glossary of dream symbols at the very beginning, though it is a great temptation to search for one.

When taken literally, the dream may speak impossible things. As people tell their dreams, they often say, "Of course, this could not happen." It could not happen literally, but the dream speaks in symbolic language. I have not yet found an artist who can paint the picture of Joseph's second dream in which he said, "The sun and the moon and eleven stars were bowing down to me" (Genesis 37:9). Literally, we cannot paint it, but we can understand it, for our dreams carry us beyond the three-dimensional world. So we must move beyond the literal objects of the dream to the story portrayed by them.

What are the most common symbols?

The house, of course, is one. Often it is the house of our childhood. We may be taken back there many times in our dreams because the dream is taking us back to the inner psychological house in which we lived as children. There may be happy memories that will be helpful in present situations, or painful memories that need to be healed. The mood of the dream will suggest whether the memories are good or bad.

A woman told me this dream:

I was living happily in a beautiful house. One day I discovered a door I had not seen before. When I opened it, I was surprised to see that it led into a room I did not know was there. The room had lovely furniture in it. My curiosity was aroused, and I found another door, leading to still another interesting room, this one containing objects of art. I was thrilled. How could I have lived here so long and not known about these rooms? That there could be still more such rooms fascinated me, but frightened me a little too.

The beautiful home symbolized that the woman had been happy with herself and had lived a rather full life. But then came new experiences and new insights about herself. These were the rooms of the house of the soul that she was beginning to discover. She was thrilled to learn there was much more to her personality than she had known before. Her fear stemmed from the possibility that she would discover things about herself she might not like. This woman was on a path of growth and maturity.

Automobiles are often in our dreams. In America they are the chief means of transportation and are almost always linked to men as the symbol of their egos.

I had the following dream:

I was driving a big new car through the countryside to a small town where I was stopped by a police officer who said the car had to undergo an inspection. This inspection was to be very thorough, even taking the motor apart and looking at it. I was disturbed because I knew the inspection would be time-consuming but I was confident that the car was new and good.

This dream came after my soul had found a new expression of freedom, represented by the big new car. The police officer in the dream stood for the authority figure in me, probably a conscience that had been so long under the bondage of rules. This authority demanded a very thorough inspection, even taking apart the machine (the organizational part of my thinking). Though I begrudged the time, I was confident of my new freedom.

I was sitting in the backseat of our car, and there seemed to be a woman driving. The windshield wiper was stuck by a big blob of ice. I came to the front seat and reached around and loosened the wipers.

When someone is driving a car in a dream, it usually suggests that the driver is in control of his life at that time. Here, I was in the back seat, and someone else was in control of my life. When my vision was blocked by the frozen condition of things, I felt the need to get back into the front seat and take control.

People are a common symbol in our dreams. Yet the most frequent mistake of dream interpretation is to take these dreams literally. Over ninety percent of the time the people we dream about relate to something in ourselves.

While talking to a group of African pastors in Zaire several years ago, I stressed this point, that the people in our dreams are almost always just symbols. They were surprised, for their witch doctors had a totally different approach. "When we dream that someone has harmed us, we tell the witch doctor our dream and he puts a curse upon that person identified in our dreams," they explained. Later they agreed that it was wrong to blame a person for a role he unwittingly played in someone else's dream.

People are more clearly delineated in dreams than are animals, so that the dreamer can more clearly see his reflection in them. Such was the case the night I dreamed

of a boyhood friend whom I had not remembered for a long time.

When I awakened I wondered why I had dreamed of him, for I knew that he represented a part of me. He was the most dogmatic fellow I had ever met.

"Surely I am not like that," I said to myself. But as I stopped to listen to my dream I remembered that just recently I had been arguing dogmatically with a friend. The dream, reflecting that part of me, was saying, "This is the way you look."

When we have dreamed of someone, two questions should be asked: First, what does he represent to me? That is, what is the basic, immediate impression of him that comes to me? Second, what is he doing in the dream that I am doing in real life?

If I dream of a president, king, or emperor, that may speak of a quality of leadership or greatness in me. If I dream of crooks, cowards, or liars, they represent parts of me too. In either case the dream is not to exalt nor condemn. The dream simply tells me that a part of me is out of balance. When I recognize the imbalance, I can then deal with it by giving that part of me to God. Thus the dream provides a real opportunity for growth.

Another common figure in our dreams is one Dr. Jung calls the "Shadow." This is a figure which represents a part of us that has been neglected or ignored and needs developing. Often the shadow appears as the very opposite of what we think we are: a strict, moral person may dream of the drunkard or prostitute. And the one who has no moral standards will dream of a saintly person. At first we might think these people in our dreams do not represent us! However the dream shows us areas in our lives that with our conscious mind, we do not know are there.

Treasure is another common symbol. Sometimes the treasure is represented by money or by a wallet that we find.

> *I was in an antique shop on the second floor of a house where someone was selling brass antiques in old paper sacks, with three pieces to a bag. When I peeked into one bag, I saw a brass harp with frayed strings. I considered the harp to be of great value and quickly closed the bag and bought it. After the woman at the counter took my money, she wanted to look inside the bag, but I said, "No, I have bought it as marked." I was afraid she would want the harp back if she saw it, so I ran down the stairs with her after me. Then I awakened.*

The dream referred to the Book of Revelation, which I had been reading. In it, I had found some old treasures, the brass antiques of the dream. The paper sacks spoke of the flimsy containers I had for these treasures, containers that were probably old and inadequate outlines of Revelation which I had done before, not worthy of the treasures they held. The number "three" often refers to something new, as it did here. The brass harp suggested the picture from chapter 14 of Revelation that I had been reading. The woman in the dream represented that part of me which did not want to sell the treasure to another part of me, my ego or my conscious self.

This dream was significant to me because through it I heard God say that I needed to take my beliefs (treasures) out of old, legalistic, traditional containers. I was to show them to the creative part of me which was now under the Holy Spirit's direction.

Money sometimes suggests energy, at other times power, as it enables us to buy what we need. The loss of a wallet with its identification cards may speak of the loss of one's identity.

Clothes, too, are a common symbol in dreams. What we wear tells others how we want them to see us—casual, formal, neat, traditional, or perhaps very rigid, as in a military uniform. The clothes in the dream reflect this inner feeling.

With no shirt on, I was lecturing before a group.

When I awakened and was writing down the dream, I asked myself what had made me uneasy or embarrassed, because lecturing without a shirt would embarrass me. After a moment's reflection, I had the answer. The audience to which I was then giving a series of lectures included in its numbers an expert in an area about which I was not well informed. I was ill at ease for fear he would disconcert me with his questions.

Clothes, and sometimes the lack of them, in dreams tell us how we are relating to people. Are we "dressed to kill" in a dream? If so, that may be our heart attitude. We may be wanting to get all the attention and through it destroy others.

Are we casually and comfortably dressed in the dream? Then we may feel comfortable in real life.

Are we stark naked? This may mean that we feel totally exposed before others. Or it could mean that we are hiding nothing from God or from those to whom we appear in the dream.

Sex. Some of the most confusing dreams are sexual ones. They are often misunderstood because of the sex symbols involved, even though sexual dreams are usually not speaking of the physical experience of sex at all. Since God intended sexual relations to be the most intimate physical union of man and woman, the sexual dream is often used to describe the intimate union of the masculine and feminine parts of the personality (see chapter 10).

Unfortunately, the person who has turned over his imagination to lustful thoughts becomes so dominated by them that no creative thought, especially one represented by a sexual symbol, can come via the dream. Preoccupation with sex raises it to the level of a false spirituality or idolatry, blocking the normal channel through which God operates in dreams, thereby preventing Him from showing the dreamer an imbalance that needs correction. When sexual fantasies take hold of a person, he needs to repent of such thoughts in order to be released and forgiven so the creative channel can be open again.

Some erotic dreams are innocent expressions of a proper physical release. Thus the nocturnal emission or "wet dream" may simply be brought on by abstinence from normal sexual relations. In the dream, the physical and sensual parts are attempting to balance themselves with the intellectual and intuitive parts of man. Lack of understanding of the normality and function of this kind of dream often produces false guilt.

Sometimes a dream will picture a sexual union between the dreamer and an alluring woman who represents the feminine or creative part of himself. Or a woman in the developmental process of her personality might dream of being wooed by a man. These dreams are usually not speaking of an adulterous relationship but using the sexual act as a symbol of the higher union between the conscious and the creative parts of the personality. When such dreams are understood, instead of bringing guilt, they bring great joy in the fulfillment of that aspect of personality growth.

The homosexual has a type of dream that needs proper understanding. A homosexual male will often dream of other young men whom he greatly admires. In his dream, he may kiss them, embrace them, perhaps have phallic fantasies with them. Such dreams are saying that the dreamer is trying to relate to a lost part of himself and to be integrated with his true sexuality or masculinity. But he will never find that lost part of himself through a homosexual relationship with other men. Instead, he needs to learn how he has lost that part of himself and seek healing.

Wars and *battles* are often in our dreams.

I was on a ship at a naval station when the captain saw an enemy vessel approaching. Everyone prepared for battle. Then a line of old battleships came by, one after another, right near our ship. We shot at them at close range, and a great naval battle began.

This dream had nothing to do with naval warfare. It spoke of the battle going on inside me, relating to my need to be aggressive at the right times. Dream pictures often come from the memory of things we see and hear, but the message is about the inner condition of the soul.

The circle and square are natural symbols which may speak of wholeness. Colors may give added meaning to symbols: red could represent anger, danger, blood, or life in the dream. White is likely to speak of purity. Though these are elementary interpretations, they were helpful to me in my studies.

Water is a frequent symbol in dreams and has many variations. Often I am beside a river, or crossing a stream. From the Bible, I learned that a river can be a source of life, as the river that watered the Garden of Eden (Genesis 2). The Nile is often referred to as the source of life for Egypt. Or water may be a healing stream, (Ezekiel 47:9—12, Revelation 22:1—2) from which our Lord invites us to drink (John 7:37—38).

Since Jesus spoke of the fountain from which the rivers of living waters flow, the dream may picture first the trickle, then the brook, and then the mighty river that flows into the sea. In a dream, the vast ocean usually refers to the deep unconscious part of man. In the sea of the unconscious, one may find good fish to eat, or encounter sharks that threaten to devour him.

There may be a ship sailing on the ocean, signaling life on the surface above the deep unconscious; or storms may appear that sink the ship. We may find treasures in the sea, suggesting a transformation process in which valuable treasures can come out of disaster or tragedy.

The different dreams that relate to water are endless.

Some little boys about four or five years old were playing in the clear water in a box about four feet square on the ground. I sent them away. Then I turned and saw them happily saying, "Praise the Lord," because one of their friends had been saved. It was beautiful.

There was more in the dream than I understood at the time. The clear water spoke of something good, like the water of life with which I was often occupied. However, the water was contained in a box, which suggested that it was within some kind of structure, as in a framework of doctrine. Even though the children were happy and loving in the water, I was still afraid of it and sent them away. I remembered the fears I had when I first began to venture into areas of spiritual renewal.

I was trying to float a big log on a little stream about three feet wide. It was hard to direct the log around the curves.

In this dream, the water was such a little stream, I could easily have stepped over it. The log was formerly a tree, symbolizing raw material that would become construction lumber in the same way that a living experience can develop into a religious doctrine. I was attempting to use the stream to carry freight that was too big for the little stream. The stream of life inside me had not grown and matured sufficiently to support the big problems that I was trying to put into it.

I was in my swimming suit, carrying a white ball, much like a pool ball, beside a very large and wide stream. Two young fellows appeared. They wanted to take the white ball from me, so I tossed it into the stream. Then I jumped after it, and they with me, with their clothes on.

This dream told me I was still beside a very large and wide stream. Evidently it was the river of living waters flowing through Christendom at that time. I was hesitant to jump in. The ball represented wholeness, and the white, purity or perfection. As a white ball is used to start a game of pool, the white ball symbolized the key to action and movement. In throwing the ball into the stream, I was moving toward involvement in the stream of living waters.

In other words, the hurt of the rejection by the Michigan church was being thrown off. By allowing God to lead me into new situations, I was moving toward maturity.

10

The Male and Female
Parts of Us

In my dream described earlier (chapter 2), I shot my mother on the stairs and upon waking was horrified at myself. How could I have done such a thing!

The interpretation given me then was that I wasn't trying to hurt my mother; she represented the feminine part of me, my gentle nature, which I was trying to squelch. I found it hard to accept the psychological dream principle that all of us, both men and women, have inside of us masculine and feminine natures. Yet this is a basic principle necessary for understanding and interpreting our dreams.

We men can rail against it all we want, but there is no getting around the fact that each of us has both masculine and feminine qualities in our personalities. When a man denies his feminine or gentle self, he will be strong but cruel. If the feminine trait dominates him, he becomes too gentle, and in extreme cases tends toward homosexuality.

It works the same way with women. Mannish females greet us today in many situations; some women seek to obliterate the differences between the sexes, demanding equal rights in all things. Most men and many women are antagonized by this aggressiveness. Yet if this masculine part of a woman is denied, she tends to become too placid and overly sentimental. The best description I know of a well-balanced woman is found in Proverbs 31:10—31, where she is portrayed as feminine but strong.

Dr. Jung called the feminine quality in man the *anima* and the masculine quality in woman the *animus.* The feminine in man and the masculine in woman need to be brought into balance so that they can lead to creativity.

Let's see how it works out in the dreams of some men and women.

A professor who appeared to others as rigid and harsh, suppressing the feminine part of his nature, had this dream:

I was walking along a street when a girl turned and kicked me, seeking to get my attention. At first I ignored her, but then I began to talk to her, which was not good, for soon she was trying to seduce me.

The interpretation worked out for him was that first of all this dream reveals his self-centeredness. The girl was not trying to seduce him as he thought, but only trying to get his attention. He needed her, but did not know it. Later he dreamed again of this same woman, only now she appeared in a different form:

A glamorous woman lived up a steep mountain behind our house. I went to her house and happened to mention the names of my daughters. She said she knew my daughters and would be glad to come down to our home for a visit. She and a man—I think it was her husband—came down and helped us in a very friendly way.

This dream indicated that the man's feminine quality was not as suppressed as it appeared to be, but was willing to come down to the level where he lived.

The next time he climbed up the mountain to see the woman, the man revealed a different feminine quality:

While climbing high up a mountain, I suddenly came upon a cave which turned out to be the home of an Indian family. A

*woman came to the opening of the cave to meet me. Behind
her lay an old woman who I thought was dead until she
stirred. The first woman then talked very intelligently to me;
she may be able to help me in a class I am about to teach.*

The Indian family represented the primitive part of the feminine
quality in him. It had been there a long time. This new quality was
intelligent and helpful, and the professor was beginning to relate to
her properly.

My efforts to suppress the feminine (creative) side of me resulted
in the following dreams:

*I spent the day with a woman about 35 years old. She was a
conservative type, intelligent, and seemed to be a nurse. I was
a doctor about her age. It was a good day, and at the end of it,
she and my wife, Lillie, got into the backseat of a Volkswagen
car I was driving. Suddenly I stopped, turned around, and
said to the nurse, "You will marry me, will you not?" She was
quiet, but seemed to respond favorably.*

Then I dreamed again:

*I saw a rainbow before me, reaching overhead and above
me. It seemed to be three colors—red, blue, and green. Each
color was like a thick rope, and they were braided together. It
was so amazing that I called Lillie and others to come and
see it.*

When I awakened and wrote down this dream, I wondered,
"Should I tell Lillie?" If the dream had occurred before our coming
to the Institute, I probably wouldn't have. It appeared that I was
not only an unfaithful husband but also an unfeeling one. Yet we
both had learned that the people in a dream like this represented
parts of me.

With some help from the analyst, we concluded that the first part of the dream, my proposal to the nurse, indicated my acceptance of the creative and good feminine part of me that she represented. In other words, I was making progress in my inner struggle to accept my feminine-creative side, while still seeking to be aggressive in leadership on the proper occasions.

The second part of the dream referred to God's covenant protection of me. In this case, we decided that the red symbolized love, the blue peace, and the green spoke of growth. That they were braided together reminded me of the Scripture that says a threefold cord cannot easily be broken (Ecclesiastes 4:12).

Lillie, of course, was more than a little curious about why she was there as a spectator when I proposed to the nurse. The answer was that Lillie was observing the development of my personality with a marriage of its various parts. My coming into wholeness, and into a better balance of my masculine and feminine qualities, could only bring a deeper relationship between us. The beautiful rainbow in the dream was God's confirming seal upon the proposal.

Properly handled, the interpretation of dreams can bring a balance and wholeness in people. In King David of the Old Testament, we see a good example of masculine and feminine qualities in proper proportion. He had towering masculine strength as a soldier and warrior, while his feminine side got him into some trouble. When his son Absalom, who had tried to take over David's throne, was killed in battle, David wept so excessively that it almost turned his victory into defeat. Joab, his general, who had about him very little feminine quality, had to help David out of his predicament (II Samuel 18,19).

A study of the life of Jesus shows us the perfect balance of strength and gentleness. In fact, it is a very helpful exercise to read through the Gospels, noting the balance between the authoritative strength and the quiet gentleness of Christ.

While most men tend to resist their tender (feminine) qualities, women by nature have resisted their creative (masculine) side—at least until the last decade or so. Women have often been trained to be submissive. This is proper up to a point, but when the woman crushes the creative part of herself, her subconscious will object, because she is out of balance.

The following is the long and detailed dream of a woman we'll call Ann who was dominated for years by her husband. We learned that this husband took the Bible teaching on male authority out of context to make her submit to him in every way.

I was working in a hospital with a doctor. We were on a balcony and saw the police shoot down a whole group of men, a musical group. The doctor, who was a kind man, was upset. "The police shoot everything and anyone and don't care," he said.

The scene shifted. I was sick in one of the hospital beds. The doctor came and sat on my bed. For some reason I still had on my clothes. Because I was so weak, the doctor helped me put on a sweater over my blouse. He was kind and gentle, and I knew he loved me and I loved him, but our relationship was always respectful. He never touched me in any lustful way.

The scene shifted again. I was now hurrying to get beds ready for all the musicians who had been shot. I was holding pieces of bedding very carefully. "You're too clean and fussy," the doctor said angrily. "Come on, let's get going." I had never seen him this way before. I was concerned that the bedding be clean, because the musicians were wounded, and I didn't want germs to infect them. He immediately felt repentant and came over and said, "I am sorry." Gently, he kissed me on the cheek.

I went to a drawer and took out a Bible. The doctor noticed and said, "I read that."

"I read it all the time," I replied. "I'm now at Hebrews 6:9."

The doctor then gave me a present, a large rubber plant, and told me I could grow it outside.

"Can't I put it in my house?" I asked. I also wanted to invite him to our house some night for dinner, but knew I would have to be careful not to let my feelings for him show, or my husband would be angry. I really loved this man, but had never told him and he had never told me. We just knew it.

*The scene changed. I was now at home, and the phone was
ringing. I answered it downstairs. It was from the doctor, who
was in an airplane which was about to crash and kill him. I
knew this somehow, just as I knew that the engines were
damaged.*

*Suddenly the doctor began saying, "I love you, I love you."
He had never before told me that.*

*I whispered back on the phone, "I love you, I love you,"
but I knew he couldn't hear me because my family was
making so much noise.*

*I ran to the upstairs phone away from the noise where the
family couldn't hear me and said "I love you, I love you." My
feelings were so real, so deep. This time he heard me, and I
knew I was comforting him. Then I said, "Do you know
Jesus? Have you invited Him into your heart?"*

*He said he had. Then the noise of the engines stopped, and I
could hear the plane crash. It was all over; there was dead
silence on the phone. I cried.*

*My sister had come upstairs and heard what I said to the
doctor, but I knew she would keep my secret. I felt the one
good thing in my life had died, but that was necessary so I
wouldn't commit adultery. I was being protected. Though I
felt deceitful in the dream because of my husband, I knew the
doctor had no deceit. His love was so beautiful, so pure, so
real, so patient, so firm, so caring and protective. My feelings
were also tender and loving.*

"When I woke up," the woman told me, "I knew the dream was
not dealing with physical adultery, but had a deeper meaning."

A dream like this is very significant because it indicates how
deeply upset Ann was not only about her marriage but also about
her own self-image. As the dream was broken down, scene by
scene, we arrived at this interpretation:

The doctor in Ann's dream was a masculine figure, representing
the authoritative, aggressive, but also creative part of her. The
dream as a whole showed the relationship between her conscious

ego and that masculine part of herself. It had nothing to do with a real-life doctor. The dream used him merely as a symbol.

In going out onto the balcony, with her creative side Ann was looking at her life from a high level. The scene before her portrayed what was going on in her inner life. She had recently been to hear a very fine musical group which delighted her. The musical group, therefore, symbolized what brought joy into her life. The policemen who shot down the musicians were authority figures (her husband) who would not allow her to accept and enjoy the creative side of her life.

The doctor, representing her masculine quality, was kind also. Proper authority can be both strong and kind. When the doctor complained about the police action, it meant that the creative part of Ann was hurt by the authority figures within her who destroyed the music in her life. Because of this, she experienced inner conflict and deep disappointment.

Ann is a person who has trouble enjoying herself, because she has an inner authority which says she cannot be both conscientious and happy. That old authority, illustrated by the policemen in the dream, destroyed the joy that wanted to spring forth within her. The doctor represented a new kind of authority, which also contained love.

The setting in the hospital bedroom indicated that the dream was entering the privacy realm of her life where none but the most intimate could enter. She was wearing regular clothes in the dream, which meant that the dream was not speaking of her work as a nurse, but of her everyday life. Clothes are symbolic of our relationship to others. When the doctor helped her put on her sweater, the dream was saying that the masculine side of her could help her relate to other people.

The love relationship between the doctor and Ann was not adulterous, even in her heart, but was symbolic of the real love relationship between two parts of herself. The masculine or creative part that was trying to help her was good and kind and pure. Sometimes the various parts of ourselves may be in conflict, and we may be shooting at them, but in this case, there was a deep harmony between those two facets of her personality.

In the dream, Ann had to get the beds ready for the musicians who were shot; in other words, she had to prepare to heal the wounded parts of herself, the parts that make music and joy. She seemed to be fussy about that work. By nature, she was not clean and fussy, only when she was a nurse in the hospital. The doctor, her masculine quality, felt that all that conscientiousness was not necessary, but that she had too many scruples restricting the joy in her life. While one part was correcting another within her, it was all done in love. This was in contrast to the damaging self-criticism that often goes on in the hearts of people.

When Ann checked out her relationship to the doctor with the Bible, Hebrews 6:9 was significant: "But, beloved, we are convinced of better things concerning you, and things that accompany salvation. . . . " Ann was very conscientious concerning her inner relationships, and she wondered whether it was scriptural to allow that masculine, authoritative, and creative part of her to be expressed. The Scripture reassured her.

The large rubber plant the doctor gave her was a picture of growth, the rubber suggesting something that could be stretched. The dream was saying she could allow this growth in her inner life to stretch her, but she asked if she could rather keep it hidden "in the house." She was still afraid to let the creative side of her be seen, even after she knew it was kind.

The love relationship between Ann and the doctor was beautiful and pure in the dream. She wanted to invite the doctor into her house, meaning that she wanted to have more fellowship with that part of herself. However, she was afraid that her husband would be suspicious, hostile. Ann should not think of the doctor in the literal sense, but always in the symbolic.

When the phone rang, Ann was at home in surroundings where her *animus* (or creative self) was weak. The domination of her husband prevailed. The doctor was calling, but on a flight away from her. Not only was he leaving, but there was something wrong with the plane.

Desperately, Ann sought to keep this part of her from leaving through her protestations of love, but family noises and static got in the way. She rushed to another phone, and was finally heard.

Then, in deep conflict, she was almost pleading with the doctor, "Do you know Jesus?" The question was really to the creative or masculine part of herself: "Are you properly related to Jesus whom I love?"

The answer came back: "I love you. I believe as you do." Then came the crash. The plane and the doctor—the masculine or creative part of her—went down in flames.

Ann had two questions of the analyst: First, "What does the dream mean?" Second, "What should I do?"

The analyst was able to answer the first. The second was much more difficult, for dream interpretation can show the forces at work inside the dreamer and can offer a warning of dangers ahead, but it stops short of recommending specific action.

For Ann, the dangers ahead are obvious. If she continues to stifle the creative part of herself, the result could be destruction of her marriage and herself as a person. But this certainly doesn't mean she should leave her husband. While he may be dominant and cruel, he might also be contemptuous of her submissiveness. She will never know unless she confronts him with her inner misery and creative yearnings. If she shows sudden new strength, he may try to crush it, but deep down he is likely to respect it. Unless she moves to some kind of confrontation and action, however, Ann's future is dismal. In too many cases, husbands are either unfaithful to or leave their abjectly submissive wives.

There is great significance in this dream for many women today. It portrays the dilemma they often face: Is it God's command for me to fulfill my creative destiny? Or is it the command of God for me to obey my husband? She can hardly ignore either command or deal with either one lightly. In the end, God must show her the solution as she meditates upon the Scriptures and waits quietly before him.

The Bible story of Esther is a good example of the proper blending of the masculine and feminine parts of a woman. Because of her beauty, a feminine quality, Esther was chosen from among all the women of Persia to be queen. Few of the people knew that she was of a minority and hated race, Israel. God gave her a task to do which would demand masculine strength: to save her nation.

She accepted the challenge and took a stand on her faith and beliefs, even to the point of being willing to die. As a result she saved her people.

As Lillie and I shared our dreams and interpretations and sought to put this ministry into proper balance with our Christian faith as a whole, we came up with almost daily discoveries about ourselves. And as we came to recognize more of the undeveloped shadow sides of our personalities and accept them, they came out of hiding.

There was the need to admit that many times we put on a front before people, that behind our public posture we had selfish, proud, angry, cruel, lustful, jealous, and other undesirable facets of our personalities hidden in the dungeon of the unconscious. When we became able to admit this, we were not giving in to those undesirable qualities, only being honest about ourselves in order that everything about us could be brought from darkness into light.

It was then that strengths began to appear under the weaknesses that seemed so evil. Selfishness could be transformed to proper care of ourselves. Pride could be turned to thanksgiving to God who has given us all things. Anger could be changed to powerful, positive actions, while cruelty became a willingness to suffer. Lust was changed into the desire for the beauty of true love.

In the same manner, the masculine and feminine traits in woman and man seek their balance. The cruel man becomes gentle, and the effeminate man turns from lustful desires to creative expressions as the feminine quality is brought into balance in him. Likewise, the sentimental woman develops an inner strength, and the mannish woman becomes feminine as that quality finds its proper place in her. As this kind of maturation takes place in the masculine and the feminine parts, they become attractive to each other and soon a wedding takes place.

I was discovering that what God wants to do through our dreams is to bring all parts of our being into harmony and help us find the fulfillment of being a whole person.

11

Is It Biblical?

Though it was stimulating to learn about dreams in a psychological institute, Lillie soon voiced the question in both our minds.

"Are we getting away from the Bible?"

"No," I said thoughtfully. "These studies have brought me back to the Bible, especially to those areas of the Bible that we had neglected."

Lillie nodded. "That's true," she said, "but I wonder sometimes whether the principles of dream interpretation are Biblically sound?"

"They seem sound to me," I said.

"They may seem so, but shouldn't you check the Scriptures for yourself?"

She had a point, so I turned to the familiar and reliable ground on which my spiritual life had been based. The Bible was the Word of God to me and a record of man's experience with God, not just over one generation or even one century, but over 15 or 16 centuries. It was the recording of many cultures from Abraham of Ur, the early Chaldean culture, Joseph and Moses in the Egyptian cultures, Daniel in the great Babylonian empire, extensive records from the Jewish tradition down to the whole New Testament Christian influence.

Since the dreams and visions of these people had the Lord's

"covering" through Scripture, the Bible was a safe record by which to test the dream principles I was learning. Were these principles just psychological theory? Were they compatible with biblical principles?

Joseph and Daniel were the chief authorities on dreams, I decided. Each of them saved his nation because God gave him the ability to interpret dreams correctly. Since it was Daniel who illustrated most of the important principles of dream interpretation, I decided to concentrate on his Old Testament book.

Daniel was prepared for his mission by undergoing some tragic experiences in his youth. He saw his own country of Judah fall. When taken captive, he doubtless observed his parents being killed by the cruel Babylonian soldiers. Then he was carried away to a foreign nation to be a slave.

There, he was forced to study a culture steeped in pagan rites and filled with occult powers. Nevertheless, Daniel determined to keep himself under the protection of the God whom he knew. And he did. When he excelled in the studies of Babylonian science and literature, the authorities rewarded him by presenting him and his three friends to the great king, Nebuchadnezzar. At this point, God blessed Daniel by giving him an understanding of dreams beyond that of all the wise men of Babylon.

Daniel's experience indicated that *when anyone first learns about dreams through other than biblical sources, that person can and should test this knowledge against the safe principles of the Scriptures.*

Daniel's opportunity to prove himself came when Nebuchadnezzar had a dream he could not remember. Nebuchadnezzar's reason for not remembering his was not a mechanical one—he probably did not have a loud alarm clock. Nor was his reason a cultural one, as it is with us, for dreams were considered very important in the Babylonian culture. He probably didn't remember his dream because subconsciously he did not want to hear the inner voice of his soul through which the dream spoke. The king was living by the rationalistic voice of his mind, which told him to build bigger palaces, more beautiful cities, and always to think in terms of a greater empire.

Nebuchadnezzar not only demanded that his wise men tell him

the dream he could not remember, but also that they interpret it for him. They replied that only the gods could do that. When the king then ordered that all his wise men—including Daniel and his friends—be killed, Daniel went to his God in prayer and asked God to show him the king's dream and its interpretation.

A point here was important to me: God wants us to come to Him for help. A psychiatrist confided to me once that through hypnosis he could draw out many secrets hidden in his patient's unconscious. Yet he felt hesitant to use this device, fearful that he would provide information to his patient who might not be ready to hear it. How much safer it is to listen to the dream which reveals only what the dreamer is able to receive.

This is what happened with Daniel, who received from God the knowledge of the king's dream. Then he risked his life to go to the king with the information, and was not afraid to proclaim the name of his God who had revealed it to him.

Before he interpreted the dream, Daniel pointed out to the king the two kinds of information which are often revealed in dreams. First, Daniel told the king that his dream revealed *what would take place in the future* (Daniel 2:28). Secondly, he explained that *the dream would help him understand the thoughts of his heart* (Daniel 2:30, margin).

The thoughts of Nebuchadnezzar's *mind* were that he was greater than all men, his kingdom was greater than all other kingdoms, and that all men should bow before him as though he were a god. The thoughts of his *heart*, however, were that there was one God who was greater than all other gods, and this God would have a kingdom greater than all other kingdoms. The dream also told him what would happen in the future if he continued in the direction his mind was taking him.

These two kinds of information are generally revealed in our dreams today. One dream may reveal the thoughts of the heart, or be a mirror of the soul; another may reveal what will happen if the dreamer continues in the way he is going.

Some dreams will give only the first kind of information; other dreams will reveal the second also. Western man has given much attention to the mind and neglected to pay attention to the heart or the deep unconscious part of man. It is obvious that we need a balance of both the mind and the heart, the conscious and the unconscious.

Nebuchadnezzar's dream of an extraordinary statue was just what a king's dream should be, drawing much of its material from the dreamer's activities. The statue had a head "made of fine gold, its breast and its arms of silver, its belly and its thighs of bronze, its legs of iron, its feet partly of iron and partly of clay" (Daniel 2:32,33).

As statues are often built in memory of men and their deeds, Daniel pointed out that this statue was in memory of certain kingdoms, each of which would stand out in its own glory. The various parts of the body (each part a kingdom) and the metals were symbols. The order of the metals in this dream went from the most to the least important, indicating the relative importance of the kingdoms rated. Since Nebuchadnezzar was pictured as the most important, he was the head made of gold. God had given him the highest place among the kingdoms represented.

The dream pictured kingdoms not then in existence. The head of gold was the Babylonian empire of Nebuchadnezzar. The silver breast with its two arms was the Medo-Persian empire. The bronze belly and thighs the mighty Greek empire of Alexander the Great. The legs of iron and feet of clay were the Roman empire, which crushed all under its feet but later fell apart.

The dream went on to describe a strange symbol, a stone which has no value compared to gold, silver, bronze, and iron. Bible scholars see the stone as representing Christ in His humanity, contrasted to the glory of the earthly kingdoms. Then came something that suggests the truly supernatural: the stone was cut out of a mountain "without hands." This foretold the virgin birth.

Finally, the stone rolling out of the mountain crushed the magnificent statue and ground it to fine powder, which the wind carried away. The stone then grew and filled the earth, a reference to the kingdom of Christ on earth, a kingdom which will sometime in the future replace all other earthly kingdoms.

The king's dream was deeply significant because it foretold our history for thousands of years ahead. Because of the dream's complexity, however, learned men of that period were a long time interpreting it. Yet God gave Daniel all the understanding the king needed.

From deep within his soul, the king knew Daniel's interpretation was correct. "Then King Nebuchadnezzar fell on his face and did homage to Daniel, and gave orders to present to him an offering and fragrant incense. The king answered Daniel and said, 'Surely your God is a God of gods and a Lord of kings and a revealer of mysteries, since you have been able to reveal this mystery'" (Daniel 2:46,47).

After he had this spiritual experience, we would think that Nebuchadnezzar would have ordered his subjects to worship and fear God. Not so. Nebuchadnezzar was converted only to Daniel and not to God. He was persuaded that Daniel knew his God, but he himself was not ready to bow to Him.

Then Nebuchadnezzar built a huge statue, somewhat like the one he saw in the dream. He was objectifying the dream instead of subjectively looking at the message for himself. He covered the whole statue with gold, implying, perhaps unconsciously, that he was not only the head but the whole statue. Furthermore, he asked all people of his kingdom to bow to his statue, thus asserting that he would take the place of the stone that would cover the earth, according to his dream.

When Daniel's three friends—Shadrach, Meshach, and Abednego—refused to worship the statue, the angry king ordered them thrown into the furnace. But the three men called for God's protection, and the fierce heat of the fiery furnace did not burn them. Thereupon Nebuchadnezzar made another acknowledgment of the greatness of God, and again it seemed that he has been truly converted.

"Blessed be the God of Shadrach, Meshach, and Abednego, who has sent His angel and delivered His servants who put their trust in Him, violating the king's command, and yielded up their bodies so as not to serve or worship any god except their own God," said the king (Daniel 3:28).

But the king's authoritarian spirit still prevailed when he said: "Therefore, I make a decree that any people, nation or tongue that speaks anything offensive against the God of Shadrach, Meshach and Abednego shall be torn limb from limb and their houses reduced to a rubbish heap, inasmuch as there is no other god that is able to deliver in this way" (Daniel 3:29).

At this point in my study, I paused for reflection. Already, in my short counseling experience, I had encountered people who claimed to be Christian believers, but who described dreams which revealed that the true attitude of their hearts was as unbelieving as Nebuchadnezzar. *Their dreams were so often a mirror of their souls.*

Soon Nebuchadnezzar had another dream. This time he dreamed he saw a tree in the midst of the earth.

"The tree grew large and became strong,
And its height reached to the sky,
And it was visible to the end of the whole earth.
Its foliage was beautiful and its fruit abundant,
And in it was food for all.
The beasts of the field found shade under it,
And the birds of the sky dwelt in its branches,
And all living creatures fed themselves from it" (Daniel 4:11,12).

Then came the second part of the dream. An angelic watcher, descending from heaven, spoke as follows:

"Chop down the tree and cut off its branches,
Strip off its foliage and scatter its fruit. . .
Yet leave the stump with its roots in the ground,
But with a band of iron and bronze around it
In the new grass of the field;
And let him be drenched with the dew of heaven,
And let him share with the beasts in the grass of the earth.
Let his mind be changed from that of a man,
And let a beast's mind be given to him,
And let seven periods of time pass over him.
This sentence is by the decree of the angelic watchers,
And the decision is a command of the holy ones. . . " (Daniel 4:14—17).

In this part of the dream, I observed several principles I had learned: One, that there can be different symbols in dreams referring to the same thing or person. In the king's first dream, he was a head of gold; in this one, he is a huge tree sheltering and protecting his people. The meaning of the symbol is always drawn from the dream and the dreamer.

Another psychological principle observed in dream interpretation is that often dreams will serve up a warning. If not heeded, the warning can lead to calamity. In this case, the warning came to the king as a voice from heaven, which made it especially important.

From that voice, Nebuchadnezzar heard what would happen to his beautiful tree if he did not heed the warning of the dream. He didn't.

I have learned that the details of dreams are very important. As I mentioned earlier, this particular dream provides an illustration of that principle through the seemingly inconsequential phrase, "Leave the trunk with its roots in the ground" (4:14).

Sometimes a person going through great emotional upheaval may dream of being on a ship tossed by the strong stormy sea. Yet that person may see a light breaking through the clouds—a sign of hope that the storm will break.

In Nebuchadnezzar's dream, the stump of the tree with its roots being left in the ground was his sign of hope. The figure is better understood in tropical countries where a tree may be cut off nearly to the ground and yet grow again. Thus though the king might be cut down as a tree, the dream indicated that if he would get right with God, he could be restored to his kingdom again.

Daniel, in his interpretation, warned Nebuchadnezzar of what could happen, and for about a year the king walked more humbly. But soon the old arrogance and self delusion returned. History tells us that Nebuchadnezzar then did lose his mind. In those days, people who were considered insane were not institutionalized but allowed to roam as free as cattle. And Nebuchadnezzar "was driven away from mankind and began eating grass like cattle, and his body was drenched with the dew of heaven, until his hair had grown like eagles' feathers and his nails like birds' claws" (Daniel 4:33).

Though he lost his mind, it was with his heart that he was finally able to respond to God. "I . . . raised my eyes toward heaven, and my reason returned to me, and I blessed the Most High and praised and honored Him who lives forever:

For His dominion is an everlasting dominion,

And His kingdom endures from generation to generation. . .

Now I Nebuchadnezzar praise, exalt, and honor the King of heaven, for all His works are true and His ways just, and He is able to humble those who walk in pride" (Daniel 4:34,37).

In the frightening dreams of Nebuchadnezzar, as in the night-mares of many troubled people, we can see that God desires to warn us of dangers ahead. In Job 33:14—22 we are given the three ways He warns us. First, He warns us directly *by the inner voice:*

"Indeed God speaks once, *or* twice, yet no one notices it."

Second, if we don't heed the inner voice, then *God speaks through frightening dreams or nightmares:*

"In a dream, a vision of the night,

When sound sleep falls on men,

While they slumber in their beds,

Then He opens the ears of men,

And seals their instruction,

That He may turn man aside from his conduct,

And keep man from pride;

He keeps back his soul from the pit,

And his life from passing over into Sheol" (Job 33:15—18).

If man fails to listen to those warnings, the third way God gets our attention is *by allowing us to fall on the bed of pain:*

"Man is also chastened with pain on his bed,

And with unceasing complaint in his bones;

So that his life loathes breads,

And his soul favorite food.

His flesh wastes away from sight,

And his bones which were not seen stick out.

Then his soul draws near to the pit,

And his life to those who bring death" (Job 33:14—22).

After weeks of combing the passages of Scripture which include dreams, I found that the Holy Spirit had indeed guided me so that I was able to sort out the great principles of truth found among the many avenues of psychological research. Time after time there was verification in Scripture of the basic principles I had been learning. Even more important, there were no warning nudges in my spirit indicating I had strayed from the path on which God had sent me.

Now Lillie and I needed to know to what use we were to put this training.

12

Dreams Can
Deal with Fears

As Lillie and I finished up our courses at the Jung Institute and prepared for a new work, we discovered we had not overcome one relentless enemy. Fear.

In fact, we realized we had always struggled with a whole gamut of fears involving our children, our health, and our ministry to other people. Perhaps the most overriding fear was economic. When you are dependent on contributions for survival, your faith is severely tested.

Now as we looked ahead to a new work, the question constantly in my mind was, "Would I receive enough speaking and teaching invitations to support us?"

Convinced the Lord would meet our needs, we went ahead and planned a trip that would span the globe, enabling us to accept many of the invitations we had received. With much gratitude for all we had learned, we said goodbye to our friends at the Institute, to the analysts who had been so helpful, and returned to America to regroup before beginning what would be almost a year-long trip. Then I had this dream:

I saw a black figure, like one cut out of cardboard, in front of our house. I did not recognize its significance. Later I saw similar figures placed in front of all the homes on our street.

We looked outside and it seemed ominous. In fear, Lillie
started running. I ran too, but as I peeked from behind a
house, a black man saw me and sent others who grabbed me.
I realized that the city had been taken over by the blacks, and
I awakened frightened.

I did not understand the dream, and it disturbed me. Neither of
us had any racial prejudice, so the message didn't seem to involve
this. The dream was still on my mind when we attended a conference at Sheomet Farms, a retreat center outside of Boston run by
Mr. and Mrs. Kenneth Johnson. When one of the lecturers spoke
on dreams, I told him about mine.

He nodded and explained that black men in white men's dreams
often speak of their fears. Although we accept and love black
people, there can reside a fear of them deep in our unconscious. In
my dream, the fact that the black figures were made of cardboard
indicated they were not real, that my fears had no basis in reality.

"Whether this trip you are about to take is right or not, you
should not be fearful about it," he concluded.

"I need to be honest," I said. "I have had some doubts about the
trip; I guess I am 51 percent sure."

That was the truth. But as soon as I faced my doubts, recognized
and accepted them, they began to disappear.

It was fortunate, perhaps, that we received reassurance through
another dream. It came from Wes, a middle-aged businessman who
had attended our lectures and become a good friend. From the time
he was in grade school, Wes had deep fears about public speaking.
The problem continued through high school, college, and into his
adult life. If called upon to speak before a group, he would have
severe heart palpitations and a freezing of the thought process
which left him incoherent and very much ashamed. To avoid such
embarrassment, he became very clever at avoiding speaking
situations and even hiding behind the backs of others in the
congregation if it appeared that he might be called upon for prayer.
The problem came to a climax when Wes was elected an elder and
would be expected to speak occasionally to the men's fellowship of

the church, a group that included a number of intellectuals. Then Wes had this dream:

I was driving my car on familiar streets in the hometown of my youth. It had been 24 years since I had left this New England town. I brought the car to a stop along the side of the road and turned off the ignition. Suddenly, through the rearview mirror, I saw a car pull up behind me and stop. The driver was furious. Rage was written all over his face. He was getting out of his car and coming after me.

At that point, I did what any sensible man would do. I started the engine and began to drive away. The angry man, however, ran alongside my window and tried to pull the door open. The look of rage and hate on his face terrified me. Gradually, I pulled away.

I drove some distance, then stopped the car a second time and turned off the ignition. The scene was repeated. This time, however, as the angry man stopped his car behind me and began running to 'my car, I cried out, "Lord, what shall I do?"

The answer came immediately, "Confront him."

I must admit that was the farthest thought from my mind. Shaking with fear, I opened the door, jumped out, and positioned myself directly in front of the enraged man.

When he saw me there, a look of shock crossed his face, and he stopped and stared at me. Then as I watched him, he began to diminish in size before my eyes. Initially, I would have judged him to tower about six feet four inches. Within seconds, however, he was reduced to a pitiful little thing about two inches in height.

At that point, I sought the Lord again and asked, "What shall I do now, Lord?"

The answer came, "Step on him."

I did, and the dream ended.

Wes had had no trouble interpreting this dream. The angry person was his own fear of speaking. The moment he confronted the fear in the dream, it shriveled up and disappeared. This meant that Wes had to take the same kind of bold action in his life. He did so by purposely seeking out and accepting speaking engagements.

If fear is a problem, I was learning, facing up to it is the first step. Then take bold action. Our trip around the world was to provide many opportunities to test this procedure.

I had received an invitation from the 200 Wycliffe Bible translators in Peru to speak at their annual conference in Yarinacocha. We flew to Lima, the capital of Peru, then took a smaller plane over the Andes where the mountains stood out among the clouds like great dark chocolate crags, iced with beautiful white snow. Descending through the clouds, we swept over the tropical jungle to the little town of Pulcalpa.

From there, we were taken to Yarinacocha, the base of operations from which the linguists fan out to various tribes. This center was cut right out of the jungle. Everything was forever green and growing. A few birds like the beautiful macaw added a touch of bright color. Bananas grew in abundance. One huge leaf served as my umbrella once when I was caught in the rain.

I was filled with anxiety when I arrived, because the Lord had stopped me from doing heavy advance preparation for my talks to these linguists. In fact, I had received His specific guidance not to take my carefully prepared lecture notes to Peru. The first night there I had this dream:

> *I was in a boat in the Sacramento River when the boat sank completely and I had to swim. However, I could not overcome the current and get back to the shore with my group. I could see I would drown if I continued to fight against the current, so I swam with it and was soon on the other side of the river.*

The message of the dream was obvious. The Lord had already filled me with His joy and peace and the *Word* for these people. I needed only to yield myself (not buck the current), begin speaking, and the rivers of living water would flow freely. The result would be more effective than if I had planned it myself.

I spoke twenty times in ten days, and Lillie and I counseled many personally. The fears in me dissolved as I trusted God to give through me the words He wanted these people to have. What came out of me was a much more spontaneous description of the movement of the Holy Spirit today than if I had structured my talks. This did not mean I was to stop advance preparation and study for all my future engagements; however, at this point in my life, God needed more freedom in me to do His work.

Later there was a meeting with a group of missionaries in New Guinea. In this very primitive country were many little villages hidden in the hills, so separated by deep gorges that over 700 languages had emerged.

I traveled with a school inspector into territory where a man had been killed by a hostile tribe just the month before. They had broken every bone in his body and chewed out his voice box. In revenge, the other tribe had killed a boy in the next village. The missionaries in the area were working under great tension and apprehension. You could sense everywhere the spiritual darkness in this country. This is what I dreamed:

I was in a boat among the trees in the water. Breaking through a barrier of branches, I moved out into the open water of the ocean. I was far, far from shore at night, holding a tiny light like a keyhole flashlight at the end of a stick. I felt that I could be seen from a great distance.

What a reassuring dream! At the beginning, I broke through the underbrush of my confusion and got into the stream of life. This stream became a great river that flowed into the ocean. Although I was now in open water far from friendly land, wrestling with the powers of darkness, yet I was not without power. In my hand was a light given me by God which broke through the darkness. Light always overcomes darkness.

Fortified by this dream, Lillie and I moved into our work with great confidence. God's protection was obvious in everything we

did. And learning to confront our own fears helped us pass this
teaching on to others.

In Zaire, Africa, came an unusual opportunity to minister
directly to some African pastors in villages with strange names like
Boko, Moanza, Vanga, Kikonga, Sonabata. In these little towns,
the pastors had gathered, fifty at each place, reminiscent of the way
Jesus had divided the crowd into fifties at the feeding of the five
thousand. Some had come by missionary plane, by crowded cars
or buses, or by sturdy dugout canoes on streams filled with
crocodiles and hippopotamuses. Others arrived after walking many
miles on foot.

One African pastor drew me aside after my talk and told me
how hard his work was and how fearful he was that he might have
to give it up. He told us he had just had this dream:

> *I was in a canoe that was sinking. I was already up to my
> waist in water. It seemed as if I and the boat would go down
> together, but then a strange power lifted my canoe out of the
> water and carried it onto the land.*

We explained that the canoe represented him and his work as a
pastor. That he was about to sink meant that failure could lay
ahead. Yet since the dream had occurred the night before the pastor
came to the conference, the prophetic message in it was very important. If he would give himself right away to the new power he
sensed in the dream, it could save him.

He prayed with us for that power, asking the Lord to rout his
fear with faith, and he received spiritual power, which not only
saved him, but carried his ministry on mightily. At this conference,
many other pastors were also filled with the Spirit of God.

In the seminars on dreams which Lillie and I began having after
leaving the Jung Institute, the subject of fear was often raised. We
were continually asked "How do I cope with a nightmare?"

We explained that very often the *dream becomes a nightmare* when it is ignored by the dreamer. To keep that from happening, a person should write down his dream, get an interpretation, and then take the action called for.

Nebuchadnezzar, in his arrogance as king, refused to heed his dreams, and they turned into nightmares. When he finally got them interpreted and did something about them, the nightmares stopped.

A woman came for counsel because she was having frightening dreams in which someone was chasing her from one building to another.

"Who is chasing you?" I asked.

Someone with a broken thermometer in her hand—it must be a nurse," she said. "I work with a nurse. She must be the one."

"No," I said, "it is not she, but what she represents to you."

The dreamer was a very gracious, gentle woman, who had never allowed the leadership quality inside her to develop. The nurse in the dream was a very strong, aggressive woman. That part was pursuing her, wanting to be recognized. If she would accept that part of her, she would balance her gentleness and become a more fulfilled woman with inner strength.

Once again I explained that when we are chased and threatened by people or animals in our dreams, we must face them instead of running from them.

Young people and children usually need help in coping with their nightmares. One tearful teenager reported this dream:

I killed my mother with an axe.

The teenager was shocked, because she could not imagine killing her mother, especially with an axe. She was reassured that this was not a prophetic dream, but one designed to show her she was trying to "kill" that part of herself represented by her mother. In her breast, God had put the desire for the freedom which comes with maturity. But that part of her still attached to her mother wanted to be protected and controlled. These two basic desires often conflict. In this nightmare, she struck out.

At some point, the mother must die psychologically to the child so the daughter can relate to her as one adult to another and not as child to mother. Not knowing how to make this happen, the daughter felt in her heart the frustration and hatred revealed in her dream.

A little boy told me of this nightmare:

I was tied to a railroad track, and the train was coming. Then I awoke.

The boy's dream was a revealing picture of his inner fears. The track spoke of the rigid discipline of his home training. The locomotive, the huge man-made machine, represented the powerful tradition in his home, which he was trying to resist.

In a situation like this, the parents need to be advised that something is out of balance in the boy's training, usually too much discipline and not enough love and affection. Children often cannot, or may be afraid to, verbalize their fears, and the dream brings them out.

A mother said she prayed that her child would not have a nightmare. I said that was like praying he not hear the fire siren. Rather, I said, she should pray that his inner condition be healed and the fears removed. Then there would be no need for nightmares.

Another mother told how she turned her children's dreams into breakfast table conversation. These were mostly happy times, but if there were fears revealed by the dreams, she helped her children by praying with them immediately.

A frequent nightmare, especially in youth, is that of falling—going over a cliff or falling from a high place. There is an old wives' tale that if you dream you are falling and you hit bottom, you'll die right then. This is not true, of course. A dream of falling usually indicates that the dreamer is not on solid ground psychologically.

If you dream you are holding onto a ledge or a shrub to keep from falling from a cliff, it may mean you are barely hanging onto a bit of growth that has taken place in your life. If you should lose your grip, you would have a fall, but it could put your feet on solid ground again.

Some have told me that they have great experiences in dreams where they are flying through the air as if they had wings. This may indicate they are trying to escape from real life and are involved in wishful thinking. Remember, every dream is personal, and the meaning of its symbols comes from the dreamer.

While some dreams about fear indicate the need of bold action to overcome the fear, other such dreams may be a warning. On our ten-month trip around the world, both Lillie and I began feeling deep fatigue and exhaustion toward the end. Then I had this dream:

I walked up to a plane that had landed at a small airport. I talked to the pilot, but he did not answer. He appeared to be in a deep coma.

The dream was disturbing. It said that I had become so exhausted that the inner, directing part of my life had ceased to function properly. Meanwhile an appearance at a big church in Auckland, New Zealand, was coming up. The next night I had another dream:

I was on the lower floor of a hospital. A medical team of doctors and nurses came into the room where four elderly patients were being sustained by life-support systems. The team had arrived to take the systems away. A nurse went to one bed and disconnected the tubes from one unconscious man. He reacted by suddenly coming to and sitting up. At this point I awakened.

This dream really alarmed me. The lower floor of a place in a dream may refer to the dreamer's physical condition, whereas the upper floor may speak of his mental state. This dream seemed to speak of my physical condition. Four being an earthly and a complete number, the four patients probably referred to my total exhaustion. The team of doctors and nurses suggested the rational part of me that was holding onto the speaking schedule which was threatening my well-being. By cutting off the life-support systems, the medical team was saying that if I continued this way I could be physically damaged.

Obviously, action was needed. I asked my host to cancel my speaking engagement in the large church in Auckland. After planning for several days' rest, I took the next step called for by this type of dream. I did not attempt to diagnose my own physical condition, but went to a doctor for an examination. Afterwards, he agreed that rest was crucial.

Careful checking needs to be done of all dreams reflecting the physical condition of the dreamer. The language is symbolic and must not be taken literally. No one should diagnose his physical condition from his dreams without consulting his physician for verification.

Once again, through my dreams God had guided me to a proper course of action. As I developed more and more confidence that God really spoke to me through dreams, my inner fears and anxieties continued to diminish.

13

I Dreamed
That I Died

A man in the prime of life came to me one day highly agitated. The dream he had the night before had upset him deeply:

I had gone to the funeral service of a friend. When it was over, I had walked up to the open casket. When I looked inside, I got a terrible shock. The body in the casket was mine!

"How do you explain that?" he asked nervously. "Does it mean I'm about to die?"

I assured him that such a dream probably *did not* mean he was soon to die. "You must look at the symbolism of your dreams," I told him. "The *you* that attended the funeral is the conscious you, the ego. The body in the casket is another part of you that has died. I cannot tell whether this is good or bad. This part may be a bad habit you have long struggled with. If so, you can say, 'Praise God, it is dead and buried.' Or it may be a good quality you have ignored so long it has finally died. Only you know the real meaning of that."

The man nodded with sudden understanding, thanked me, and left. The relief on his face indicated that he knew what part of him had died, but he didn't confide in me.

Death in a dream does not speak of a physical but a

psychological death, or death of one part of the personality. Death in a dream may be a very good thing. It can tie in with one's spiritual growth, a process Paul described so vividly: "I have been crucified with Christ; and it is no longer I who live, but Christ lives in me; and the life which I now live in the flesh I live by faith in the Son of God, who loved me, and delivered Himself up for me" (Galatians 2:20).

Just as seeds do not grow and multiply without death, so I have discovered that there is death in our every stage of maturation. The dream will picture it as the death of either another person or the death of our own selves. If I die in the dream, it usually represents the death of my ego; if another dies in my dream, it represents a different part of me. If I know the person who dies, then I may be able to know what part of me that person represents by his characteristics. If I do not know him, then I must wait and find out through other dreams.

I dreamed that a nurse told me very gently but firmly that I would die soon. I questioned this, but she was emphatic. I was disappointed that I did not know of my impending death in time to have made better preparations for my family.

This dream was saying I was to prepare to go through a psychological, not a physical death. The old ego must die, and a new one must be born. Soon after, I had the following dream that startled me:

A sum of one million dollars was given me to distribute. Each person was to get one hundred dollars. Soon I was helping some black people get their portions, particularly women who had babies. These people all had needs, and I was quite busy assisting them.

Then the scene changed to a monastery. A word was given that a certain man was about to die. The explanation was shocking: "A knife will cleave his heart." Then I realized I was that certain man. This was a blow, but somehow I knew it was right, for I was the priest, and dying was a part of the ritual. I went to say goodbye to Lillie and wondered what she would say, but knew she would agree it was right for me to die.

The first part in the dream indicated an unlimited amount of energy or power was offered to me. One million dollars seemed an astronomical sum. Each part of me was to get a little. The black people represented the unknown parts of me. The babies represented new areas of growth.

The second part of the dream showed me I must go through a psychological death. It was a ritual; in other words, the age-old death and resurrection process. I knew it was right. The knife or sword is the instrument which separates the old from the new, going deep into the unconscious realm. I was about to undergo that death process.

Four months later I had a dream which showed me this death had taken place:

I saw a car that was used to drive down through the earth. The car was operated by a pushbutton, but I didn't know how it worked. Suddenly Lillie and I and another man were being driven by the man's wife down through the earth to a grave. I wondered how the transfer from this life to the next would be made after we were down in the grave. Would the earth fall on us, or what?

I had a terrible fear the car would drive off, leaving us alone. But when we arrived, I stepped out of the car into a place like an underground garage. As I walked to a garage-like door, and started to go through it, I fell and died. As I died, I knew I was making the transfer, yet I was not quite through the doorway and was afraid the door would close on me. Then someone pulled me a little farther inside.

As soon as I hit the ground, I got up again and was ready to step into another car which was coming down through the earth for me. There were other people in the car. I stepped in, and we started off through the earth, stopping briefly in a place like an underground motel, where I saw three or four women and a man in the lobby. As I spoke to them, one of the women said she was Presbyterian, one a Methodist, and one a Baptist. Though they had wonderful smiles on their faces, they also looked as if they had died. The dream ended as we left.

This dream came at the time I was leaving the old structure of my inner life and entering the new. I had some fear of what would be involved in going into this "death," for death is still our enemy, and we do all we can to avoid it. But the transfer was pleasant, and with the help of another person, I made it without difficulty. Going through to the other side of the earth symbolized the death and resurrection of my inner life. The narrow religious parts of me seemed to have died, and new avenues of ministry were opened.

There are dreams which do foretell someone's death, but when physical death is presented in a dream, it will not usually be pictured as death, but illustrated symbolically. For example, a friend of ours had this dream:

I saw a bird flying with great speed through the air. Suddenly the bird hit a wall and dropped dead.

The next morning, the friend told several people of his dream. That afternoon he dropped dead. I'll never know for certain, but my guess is that this man had received in his dreams many similar signs that he was living at too fast a pace. His last dream was the final alarm, but it came too late.

Ted Sanford, a 75-year-old Anglican priest, was very sick and in great pain and anxiety when he had the following dream:

I dreamed of my childhood home; then I saw myself in boarding school. Next I saw my missionary parish in China, and then my parish in New Jersey. Finally I observed myself in my room, lying on my couch. I looked up and noticed the clock on the mantel had stopped at 11:00. Then I saw the mantel change into a doorway. A path of pure light came through the door. I got up off my couch and went out upon the path of light through the opened door.

The next morning Ted told this dream to his wife, Agnes, who wrote it all down as he told it. After the dream, his pain and anxiety went away, and about a week later he fell asleep in his chair and never woke up, just as he had walked away on the path of light through the door in his dream. He had foreseen his own death, and knew there was nothing to fear in it.

There have been many occasions when the Lord has used a dream to reassure us that death should not be feared, but is indeed a journey into a wonderful new life.

Helen Reesor, a friend from Waterloo, Ontario, told us one such experience. Helen is a highly respected family physician, and her husband, Glyn, was a professor of physics at the University of Waterloo and an earnest disciple of Jesus. This couple met regularly with two other couples for prayer and Bible study.

One night Glyn had a severe stroke and heart attack. The doctor's verdict was that Glyn had suffered brain damage and might never be a normal person again. Helen phoned the others in her group, asking for prayer for her husband, specifically that the Lord would either heal Glyn totally or usher him quickly through the valley of the shadow. It seemed that Glyn had once expressed fear of a lingering, painful death, but he had no fear about his future with Jesus.

At two o'clock the next morning, Glyn passed away. Helen did not phone the other members of the prayer group until nearly noon to tell them the news. That night one of the women in the group had this dream:

I saw all six members of the prayer group visiting together. Each was clearly identifiable. Glyn, however, was the largest and tallest and strongest and healthiest of them all. He was laughing as he said, "Oh! I thought I'd died!"

In "real" life, Glyn was the shortest man in the group!

14

Visions

Years ago a member of my church was sitting at her sewing machine weeping because of a sorrow that had overtaken her. Then she sensed a Presence in the room, looked up, and saw the figure of Jesus. He spoke not a word, but the love on His face so deeply moved her that a year later, when she was comforting Lillie and me, she could not speak of this experience without tears. His comforting Presence was still vividly real to her.

How do you explain something like this?

It seemed to me that the Lord so loved this woman and her gentle sweet spirit that He chose to appear in a vision and show her His love and comfort her.

There is confusion in the minds of many people between visions and dreams. In Scripture it is sometimes hard to distinguish between them. The simplest way to separate the two is to understand that *the dream comes while we are asleep and the vision while we are awake.*

Some specialists in the study of dreams have concluded that we dream 24 hours per day and that part of the brain never stops passing a series of images through the mind. Generally, we do not pick up a dream when we are awake, for the mind is occupied with its thoughts. Occasionally however, the dream breaks through our thoughts, and we have what is sometimes called a waking dream or vision.

There are several different kinds of visions. Sometimes the vision breaks through our thoughts and runs before us like a television show. At other times, it is almost as if the vision is in the imagination, where it is subtly showing us something.

I do not have visions frequently, probably because my rational mind has too much control, not allowing the vision to come forth. When a vision does come to me, it is usually not as clear a picture as it is with some. But when we were about to move to Florida in 1977, a picture appeared in my mind of the home we were to buy. The picture was of a secluded area surrounded by trees, in the center of which was a house. It was impressed on me that this was the first home we would own.

That is exactly what the Lord has given us, a lovely house in a secluded Florida village with many trees. Over 100 pine, palm, and oak trees surround us, yet we are only ten minutes from the town's shopping area and airport.

Unfortunately, it has been generally suggested that if a man sees visions, he is seeing something that is not there, since others do not see what he sees. The truth is just the opposite. Visions show us a reality that cannot be seen with the natural eye. This is clearly demonstrated through numerous examples from Scripture.

For example, when Jesus took Peter, James, and John with Him on the mountain to pray, Moses and Elijah appeared, and Jesus talked to them about His imminent departure from the earth. Peter was excited, for Moses and Elijah were just as real to him in the vision as was Jesus. Impulsively, he offered to make three sacred tents, one for Moses, one for Elijah, and one for Jesus (Luke 9:28—36).

On one occasion, three men appeared to Abraham, and he prepared a dinner for them. Later he discovered they were angels (Genesis 18). Manoah was disturbed when an angel appeared to his wife and not to him (Judges 13). According to Scripture, angels can be seen by some and not by others. The spiritual world manifests itself only as man is able and open to receive it.

Visions must be interpreted just as carefully as dreams. I spoke once on the subject of dreams and visions to a group of missionaries in a South American country. That night a child of one of the missionaries had a vision as she was preparing to go to bed:

> *A man was standing at my bedroom window with his arms outstretched. I could not tell if he looked like my father, or like Jesus, but I was afraid of him. Then he vanished.*

Her fear tipped me off that there were negative forces involved. The same girl had a second vision the following night.

> *The man I had seen in the vision before came again and pushed me down onto my bed. I was very frightened, but then he suddenly left.*

This time I was convinced that some kind of evil was involved. The devil was disguised as Jesus or her father, but his actions gave him away.

The girl's father was asked to check into the history of his house. He found that the people who had lived there previously had used it for occult practices. Now we knew what had happened. The house had been opened to demonic spirits who had moved in and were now determined to oppress the new occupants, Christian missionaries. Being unable to find a vulnerable spot in the faith of the parents, the satanic spirit had singled out their sensitive child to frighten.

The interpretation of this vision enabled the missionary parents to take quick action. A ceremony of exorcism was held during which the evil spirits were expelled from the house; the atmosphere in it was cleansed, and the parents prayed for the presence of protecting angels to keep the demonic spirits from returning.

One of the more fascinating aspects of visions is how God's protecting angels sometimes appear in them. A young mother told of one angelic encounter. Although she and her husband had been told by doctors that they could not have children, six years later she became pregnant and gave birth to a beautiful little girl, Melanie. The family lived close to a busy highway, and when her daughter started to walk, the mother was quite concerned that the very active Melanie might wander out onto the road. Knowing she couldn't watch her child every second, the mother decided to ask God to take care of Melanie at all times.

Early one morning, the mother slipped into her daughter's room, finding Melanie asleep. But something she saw so stunned her that she ran to get her husband. Then the two of them returned to Melanie's room.

"Do you see it?" she asked breathlessly.

"See what?"

"It's gone!" The mother's voice was soft with disappointment, but she was still wide-eyed. "There was a form at the foot of Melanie's bed. It was a little person, like Melanie, except its hair was gold and its head was bowed, looking down at Melanie. I know it was an angel watching over Melanie. Such a beautiful presence!"

The woman was greatly helped by this vision, for she felt God was telling her He had heard her prayer and that He loved her so much He had commissioned an angel to watch over her child. "I know God has His hand on Melanie, and that I can trust Him completely," she told me.

"A lovely story," you may say, "but why did the angel appear as a small child?" We don't understand these heavenly mysteries, but we do know that the vision is a reality we cannot see with our physical eyes. It comes at a time and place where the person can receive it.

Dr. V. Raymond Edman, former president of Wheaton College, told how he was helped by an angelic visitor. The Edmans had just arrived in Ecuador as young missionaries and were very discouraged with the slow progress of their work. One day there was a knock at the door, and young Mr. Edman answered it. A Quechua Indian woman stood at the door wearing the customary Quechua dress—a large black felt hat with the brim turned up all the way around, and a floor-length skirt gathered very full at the waist. Her blouse was bright red.

To Edman's surprise, the Quechua woman began to speak such warm words of encouragement to him that he was deeply touched and moved, like the Emmaus disciples whose hearts burned within them when they heard the words of Jesus (Luke 24:32). After speaking the encouraging words, the woman quickly left.

Dr. Edman turned from the door to tell his wife, who was in another room, about the visitor. "Invite her into the house," she said.

Quickly he turned around and bounded out the door to call her. But there was no one to be seen. He was stunned. How could she have disappeared? Instead of fences the Ecuadorians have mud walls about six feet high along the road in their villages. These mud walls have no openings except for doors into the houses. Dr. Edman said there were mud walls on either side of their house going a long way to the next house. The woman could not possibly have walked or even run out of sight in the few moments he had turned to speak to his wife. Nor did he ever see the visitor again during the years he lived in the village.

Awed, the Edmans concluded they had been visited by an angel. Why should the angel appear in the dress of a Quechua woman? Perhaps because the Edmans were at the point where they thought they would never be able to reach through to the Quechuas, and they needed encouragement from just that source.

A big step in breaking down the barriers between early Christians was brought about by a vision. Jesus had said, "I lay down My life for the sheep. And I have other sheep, which are not of this fold; I must bring them also, and they shall hear My voice; and they shall become one flock with one Shepherd" (John 10:15, 16). He wanted the barriers dropped between the Jew and the Gentile, the slave and the free, the male and the female.

But His disciples were slow to get the message. It was working in Peter's heart, however, he was reluctant to obey. One morning God put him into a deep trance so that his mind would not interfere with his heart, for it is the reasonings of our minds that often interfere with the voice of God in our hearts. Then He showed Peter a vision. In it, "the sky opened up, and a certain object like a great sheet coming down, lowered by four corners to the ground, and there were in it all kinds of four-footed animals and crawling creatures of the earth and birds of the air.

"And a voice came to him, 'Arise, Peter, kill and eat!'

"But Peter said, 'By no means, Lord, for I have never eaten anything unholy and unclean.'

"And again a voice came to him a second time, 'What God has cleansed, no longer consider unholy.'

"And this happened three times; and immediately the object was taken up into the sky" (Acts 10:11-16).

Peter clearly understood from the vision that the animals in the great net or sheet let down from heaven were not "kosher" for the Jew. They were legally unclean, and Peter still kept to the Hebrew laws. But the voice, which he knew to be the voice of the Lord, said, "Arise, Peter, kill and eat." That the vision was repeated three times was important. Peter knew he must be obedient and immediately respond to the vision. But how?

God soon showed him by sending an angel to appear before a deeply religious Roman officer and Gentile, Cornelius. The angel gave specific instructions to Cornelius to invite Peter in his home.

The next morning, Peter was told by God to go with the soldiers who came to lead him to Cornelius' house. He obeyed. When he arrived at the officer's home filled with Cornelius' Gentile relatives and friends, Peter quickly explained his position: "You yourselves know how unlawful it is for a man who is a Jew to associate with a foreigner or to visit him; and yet God has shown me that I should not call any man unholy or unclean" (Acts 10:28).

Peter's vision had nothing to do with changing the Jewish laws of nutrition; it was concerned with changing the hearts of the Jews toward the Gentiles.

So Peter preached about Jesus to those gathered in Cornelius' home. God, knowing Peter was still too prejudiced to give an altar call to the Gentiles, poured out His Spirit on them as He had done on the Jews at Pentecost.

When God deals with our problems today, He may use dreams and visions just as He did with the early Christians.

Visions sometimes foretell the future, warning us not to take a certain step, or assuring us that a planned trip or action has His blessing. My most vivid memory of such a vision dates back to some years ago when Lillie and I were about to take a trip to Rome.

Several days before we were to leave, a group of us met for fellowship and prayer. A word of direction was given. Then someone had a vision of a chalice and host. There was singing and sharing together. It was a delightful evening.

Afterward, a young student came up to Lillie and I and said, hesitantly, that he, too, had received a vision. His vision was of Rome, where doors everywhere were open to us. He saw us going through wide arches.

Always very careful about visions and prophecies of this kind, we thanked the young man, but set the vision aside for further confirmation.

Actually, we had planned only a few days in Rome, because we had very few contacts there. This was our rational and limited thinking, but God had something much bigger in mind.

I had written Father Francis Martin in advance and asked if Lillie and I could attend one of the prayer meetings held regularly in the Vatican. He kindly arranged for us to stay with the Sisters of Bethany, who give themselves to entertaining and providing tours for Protestant guests.

Bill Hood, a graduate student of the American Academy working on his doctorate in the history of art, was our guide when we visited St. Peter's Cathedral. He took us to a gathering of the core group of the prayer meeting. As we were getting acquainted, Bill inquired as to the subjects of my lectures. Among them, I mentioned the healing of memories.

"We have been praying for two years that God would send us someone to teach us about the healing of memories," he said. "But I'm sure we didn't expect God to send a Baptist minister! Will you share something on this subject at the core group meeting?"

I did, and there was such great interest that I spoke again at the Sunday meeting. Then came a request for me to give all my lectures to the core group—twelve hours of lectures and discussions.

I knew this must be of God, for I could not have managed such an invitation no matter how hard I tried. However, at that time, I was so exhausted from work and travel I had to decline.

Bill took my reply to the core group and came back with a most interesting proposal. "If we send you to a sea resort for a week of rest, could you do it then?" How could we refuse?

They sent us to Port Ercole near Orbetello, Italy. It was spring-time on the Mediterranean. Port Ercole was practically an island, with only a slender strip of land connecting it to the mainland. We looked down on the beautiful bay with blue waters. There were fishing boats and yachts in the harbor, and two views with old ruins overlooking each side of the entrance to the harbor. Nearly every day, Lillie would pack a lunch, and we would go up to a site overlooking the bay and enjoy the trees in blossom and the wild-flowers under the blue sky. We read and prayed and rested. One night I had this dream:

> *Lillie and I went into a house, but at the bedroom we came to a dead end, so we turned left and went out the side door and came into a new world that seemed like the old sections of Mexico.*

The dream gave a clear picture of my inner life. In certain ways I had come to a dead end. Spiritually, I was at the end of an old pattern of thinking and practice, which had kept me in a kind of bondage to religious institutionalism and separation. The turn left was to a world new to me, yet old in tradition and setting. The message seemed clear: I was to move freely into this new world that included Roman Catholics.

When Lillie awakened on the morning following my dream, she had a vision of many Roman arches with thousands of people coming through them as far as the eye could see, filling the whole street. This vision confirmed the vision the student had before we left on the trip.

The lectures I gave to these Roman Catholic priests, nuns, and lay people became a milestone in my spiritual journey. There was not only real fellowship and prayer together, there was a unity of Spirit and a sense of the Lord's power. I was amazed.

The doors had been opened to me by Christians of different

backgrounds and practices. In turn, my whole perspective had been enlarged, my understanding of how God works increased, and my faith strengthened. I had passed through an arch to begin a whole new ministry.

All of this began with a small vision given to a student who hesitated even to share it. It reaffirmed my conviction never to evaluate a vision until it was interpreted. And equally important, never to act on a vision unless there was confirmation. What God says to us in a vision or a dream, He will confirm in other ways, perhaps through a word from a pastor or friend, perhaps through a word from Scripture, perhaps through a circumstance.

My experience, and that of many thousands of others, is that God *does* speak to us through visions and dreams. Usually His message to us comes indirectly. On rare and special occasions, He appears and speaks to us directly in a vision or dream as He did to Abraham, Jacob, Joseph, Moses, Daniel, and countless thousands of average people down through the ages.

His overall message is: "I love you and I want to help you. Listen to Me, obey Me, follow Me, and I will bless your life."

15

Satan and the Dream

The onslaught of evil is so widespread today, we need to see how our dreams can help us wage spiritual warfare. Satan has strongholds everywhere, particularly among unbelievers. While meeting with Christian pastors and missionaries during our trip around ·the world, Lillie and I found ourselves in daily confrontation with the enemy.

For example, here is the dream of one African pastor:

> *I was in my village trying to reach out for God, but I could not get through to Him because some little men were hindering me. All my efforts to break through to God were of no avail. Then, strangely, a ladder was set up for me, and by the use of that ladder, I was able to reach God.*

The first picture was clear—there was unrest in the pastor's village setting, and he was having difficulty trying to get through to God. When asked who were the "little men" hindering him, the pastor said he thought they were pygmies. But we recognized that was a rational explanation. We had to get the meaning of the "little men" symbol from the culture of Africans themselves.

The answer came when we happened to visit another village

several days later. The people were friendly, and the chief himself met us at the entrance to the village. There he showed us a small hut about two feet high, obviously a sacred spot. The chief explained that when one of their men died, the village leaders would cut a small branch, carefully peel off its bark, and place it in the little hut. These branches or sticks were called "little men."

The chief explained that when the men of his village went out on a hunt, they made an offering at the little hut for the success of the hunt. When the hunters presented their offerings, they were worshiping the spirits of the dead. They called this native witchcraft their "kindoke."

Suddenly, enlightenment came. It was the witchcraft represented by the "little men" of his dream that was keeping the pastor from reaching God. Perhaps their "kindoke" was carried on partly in innocence, partly in fear, or perhaps secretly to appease the powerful witch doctor, but the dream revealed this was what kept the pastor from getting to God.

The next significant symbol of the pastor's dream was the ladder. Immediately we were reminded of Jacob's dream in the Bible. When Jacob had tricked his brother and had to run away for his life, the record says, "And he had a dream, and behold, a ladder was set on the earth with its top reaching to heaven; and behold, the angels of God were ascending and descending on it. And behold, the Lord stood above it and said, 'I am the Lord, the God of your father Abraham and the God of Isaac; the land on which you live, I will give it to you and to your descendants'" (Genesis 28:12, 13).

This biblical story was very significant to the African pastor. It told him that even though he had allowed satanic witchcraft to hinder him, God would honor the desire of his heart and put up a ladder for him to get to God. The ladder represented the power of God over witchcraft.

We showed the pastor that Jesus had defeated Satan when He died on the cross, that today we can stand against all the efforts of the enemy by claiming this power that Jesus makes available to those who are committed to Him.

By accepting these teachings, the pastor was able to get through to God in a new way. But without the dream interpretation, we would have never known the real problem.

It is important to remember that while the capacity to dream comes from God, Satan can get into our dreams. When this happens, there is a surefire way to get him out of the picture. Simply say, several times if necessary, "I rebuke you, Satan. Be gone in the name of Jesus."

During our trip to a New Guinea mission, we ran into a family situation where Satan had secured a real toehold. A village husband had this dream:

I was fishing in a stream and caught fish after fish, but they were little fish, and they were all dead.

The village witch doctor had interpreted the dream to mean that the man's wife would have no living children. Perhaps by the power of suggestion, enforced by witchcraft, the dream's interpretation had come true. Three children were born to the woman. All were stillborn or had died shortly after birth. The woman had become known as the woman who could not have living children.

We arrived in the village at a time when she was pregnant again. The baby was expected in a few weeks, and the woman was in deadly fear for her child and even for herself. The villagers believed that a curse had come upon her.

When the missionaries asked me for advice, I suggested they pray for the woman, setting her free from the bondage of the dream interpretation by the witch doctor. They agreed to do it, and invited Lillie and me to help them. Late one afternoon, we were led through the jungle to a tiny thatched-roofed hut where the woman was to bear her child.

In fear and trembling, the woman looked up at us from a mat on which she was sitting. The setting was stark: dirt floor only partially covered by thatch, and little else to provide any comfort.

We laid hands on the woman and prayed for her by the authority of Christ, cutting her free from the bondage of fear. In the same way, we sought deliverance from the curse imposed by the witch doctor, while the woman stared at us in wonder and gratitude.

The next morning came spectacular news! A healthy baby boy had been born to the woman, and she could hardly contain her joy. Within a matter of hours, she was up and moving about the village, showing how we had laid hands on her and prayed for her and how wonderfully the baby had come. The curse had been broken, and she was free.

There was nothing wrong with the husband's dream, but the wrong interpretation had given Satan domination over the woman's mind and heart. God's power will always rout Satan when we call upon Him.

16

Final Guidelines
to Dream Interpretation

A pastor in Canada invited me to become involved in his program. The offer was tempting. Sensing that it might lead to an important work, I wrote him, expressing interest and asking for more specifics. Then Lillie and I prayed that God would reveal whether going to Canada was His will for us. Shortly thereafter, I dreamed as follows:

Some children were playing in the shallow end of a river or lake. I thought the water was several feet deep, so I made a flat dive into the water. But the water was only six inches deep, and I hit my head on the bottom and rolled over with my face up. My face was out of the water, but I could not move. Then I awoke.

Lillie and I had no trouble interpreting this dream. Some years before, I had dived into a lake I thought was at least six feet deep. It proved to be only two feet deep, and I hit my head hard on the bottom, nearly breaking my neck.

This dream was a warning. If I moved too quickly (plunged headfirst) by acting on my rational instincts, I would be hurt. The offer was approached very cautiously, more questions asked, prayers continued.

The big attraction for me was the opportunity to reach many people, but as more information came through about other conditions, we knew the invitation was not God's will and turned it down. Later we discovered that the situation would have been totally wrong for us. God answered our prayers through my dream.

Ever since we jumped into the stream of His living water, God has blessed us. When I was dismissed from my church and faced an uncertain future, He comforted me and led me into a new and exciting ministry. When we were out of funds, He provided for us in surprising ways. When we were fearful, He calmed us. When we were headed in the wrong direction, He commanded our attention and put us back on the right track. When we were uncertain about our teaching procedure, He showed us where we were wrong. When our faults got in the way of our work or our relationships with others, He corrected us.

God did all this through our dreams. He reaches us and teaches us in other ways, of course, but we have deepened our relationship with Him tremendously through our openness to hear Him through our dreams.

He will speak through dreams to anyone who sincerely seeks His help. If you want God to guide you and your family through dreams, here is a summary of our suggestions on how to proceed:

1. *First, make the basic decision* that you want and need God's help and direction for your life, and second, that one way you'll seek it is through a determined effort to find His guidance through your dreams.

2. *Keep a note pad beside your bed and write down the dream the moment you awake.* Don't try to decide the value of the dream before you understand it. Write down all its details, no matter how insignificant they may seem to you.

3. *Remember that the dream speaks symbolically.* Seek to find associations for each symbol of the dream. For example, if a house appears in your dream, does it remind you of your childhood home? If so, then the dream may be carrying you

back to an experience that originated there. Or does the house remind you of one that you built, where you had so much fun in constructing something worthwhile? If so, the dream may encourage you to begin the restructuring of your inner house. List all the associations until you find the one that feels right.

4. *Look at the setting of the dream.* What were you thinking about, or in what were you emotionally involved when you had the dream? For example, a woman seeking to improve her relationship to her husband had the following dream:

> *I was riding a motorcycle in heavy traffic and kept cutting in and out of it until, finally, I almost caused an accident.*

Questioning brought out that a marriage problem deeply troubled the woman. She got so irritated over her husband's slowness in speaking that she often interrupted him. She also admitted she was impatient over his hesitancy in making decisions.

When I pointed out that if she kept on "cutting in" on her husband, there would be a blowup (accident) in the marriage, she agreed to face the situation and try to change. The husband-wife setting of the dream was the key to its interpretation.

5. *Remember that most dreams are subjective. The experts estimate that 95 percent of all dreams have something to say to the dreamers about themselves, even if the dreams are about someone else. Only 5 percent are objective, or really refer to other people being dreamed about.* Objective dreams are usually about those who are closely related to us and with whom we are emotionally involved. (Daniel was deeply involved with Israel and the surrounding nations and so dreamed objective dreams about them.) As much as we would like to have it, there is no rule by which we can tell whether a dream is objective or subjective. It is usually best to try the dream on subjectively to see if it is speaking about

yourself. If it is not, then listen carefully to see what the message is saying and how you are to relate to the person involved.

I've learned that when I dream about Lillie, I must be careful to observe whether my dream is objective or subjective. It may be telling me that the feminine part of me is out of balance again. (See chapter 10.)

Even if there is strong indication that you are dreaming about someone else, and your dream really does concern that person and not you, the necessary action may still need to come from you. The dream may be a call for you to pray for that person, or to relate to him in other ways. Be careful about telling others you dreamed about them, however, for this can be destructive. You may even be projecting your problems upon them.

6. *Don't strain to get the message of your dream.* Sometimes the message will be obvious. Often the dream will defy interpretation. Don't be discouraged. Keep recording your dreams, even if you don't understand them. When you reread them in sequence, often a pattern will emerge. There is a sequence in dreams, and one dream may be only one scene, like one frame out of a whole movie. If deeply frustrated, seek out experts for help. Some dreams may not be understood for years, but in time, as you let the dream and its associations rest in your mind, the light will come, and you will say, "Aha! I see it!"

7. *When an interpretation comes, test it four ways* to be sure of its accuracy: (a) Go directly to God in prayer for confirmation, remembering that God speaks to us in different ways, dreams being only one of them. (b) Check Scripture, since God doesn't contradict Himself by saying one thing in the Bible and the opposite in a dream. (c) Seek confirmation from trusted friends and associates. (d) Heed the feeling you have in your own spirit about the interpretation. Even if you don't like the message, the truth of it will usually plant itself in your heart.

8. *Take the action called for by the dream.* God is constantly seeking to change us. We tend to resist. If He tells us through a

dream to do something, and we confirm the interpretation as outlined above, not to take action is deliberate disobedience. Such disobedience would place our relationship with God in jeopardy.

Now let's assume that you've made some progress in dream interpretation and might even be considered an authority by some of your friends. They will bring their dreams to you for analysis. What should you do?

• Resist the temptation to interpret another's dream until you've spent at least five years learning to understand your own. Sharing dreams with others during this period can be valuable, but do it in the role of seekers, not authorities.

• If you feel God's blessing on your understanding of dream interpretation, interpret dreams for others with the awareness that God alone can help you understand a dream well enough to present the interpretation to another.

• The dream speaks to Christians and non-Christians alike. It will eventually lead each man to God and do so in a timing which the dreamer can accept. Therefore, follow both the dream's direction and timing with the dreamer.

• Never impose your interpretation on another. Always draw out the meaning of the dream from the dreamer. Ask the dreamer what the symbols of the dream mean to him or her. Never take the validity of your interpretation for granted. Watch for the dreamer's recognition of the right interpretation. The powerful king, Nebuchadnezzar, recognized Daniel's interpretation of the dream to be correct though it warned of God's judgment. Realizing the accuracy of his captive's interpretation, Nebuchadnezzar immediately elevated Daniel to a high position. The same thing happened with the great Pharaoh of Egypt when his dream was interpreted by a Hebrew prisoner, Joseph. And in the same way, you too must wait for the dreamer's recognition of your interpretation. If your interpretation doesn't "click" with him or her, drop it.

• Do not attempt hasty interpretation of dreams that come over the telephone or by letter unless you have an intimate knowledge of the dreamer's life. Impulsive or superficial interpretation can be harmful.

• Finally, if you have a dream or vision involving another person, pray for guidance as to whether you should reveal it to the person—and how. Always let the other person have the final right of interpretation.

Someone had a vision for Lillie and me when we were speaking to a Mennonite group in Ontario, Canada, about five or six years ago. We had become weary of traveling and were longing to settle down in the right location and with the right house as our base. The rolling country near Kitchener, Ontario, with its well-kept farm lands, and houses tucked into the woods, seemed ideal. At that time, our furniture was stored in a friend's home in Flint, Michigan.

During the series of lectures I gave to the Mennonites, a friend called us from Michigan to say he had found just the right house for us, one tailored to our special needs, which we had described to him earlier. He was so sure the house was right that he offered to send a small plane to fly us to see it.

Since both Lillie and I had doubts about the proposed house, I decided to try an experiment that evening with my group of seventy-five. I spoke on the subject of listening. At the end of my presentation, I suggested that we all listen to God together on one matter: Were Lillie and I to fly back to Michigan the next day in that small plane to look at the house? We waited for about five minutes in prayerful but expectant silence; then the answers began to come through:

"In quietness and confidence shall be your strength."

"Except the Lord build a house, they labor in vain that build it."

Twice this word came: "God does not usually rush into things."

"Simply trust in God, day by day."

The responses confirmed our inner feelings that we were not to rush back to Michigan to look at the house.

Then a woman in this group told us privately of a vision she had for us:

The picture of a big beautiful green maple tree filled my vision. In fact, I could hardly see around it because it was so big. I strained very hard until finally I was able to look around the tree. When I did so, I saw that the Lord was behind the tree.

Was the vision for us? If so, what did it mean? I concluded the vision was for us because of my unusual request of these people.

With the maple leaf being so prominent in the flag of Canada, the woman thought the vision meant we should live in that country. But suddenly a surprising interpretation came from within me and I knew it was right: "Canada has so filled your vision, you cannot see the Lord any more!"

Since the vision had been given for me, I had the final right of interpretation. My interpretation was later confirmed in several other ways, including the fact that the right place for us turned out to be in another location.

In conclusion, let me stress again that there are no easy routes to dream interpretation. The dream has a language of its own, and it takes time and effort to learn how to use that language. We can no more expect to master dream interpretation quickly than we can expect to speak another language correctly the first time we attend class.

Since the meaning of the dream comes through symbols, everyone interested seeks a glossary of terms. Nothing really helpful is available, because each symbol has so many different meanings. The real meaning of the symbol of each dream can be obtained only from the dreamer.

Despite the difficulties, the rewards that come from understanding one's dreams are enormous. The dream is the mirror of the soul, revealing what goes on in one's inner life. We've discovered that the dream throws light into dark areas, gives encouragement to weak parts of the personality, deflates the ego, and builds up the true self. There is no better way to get to the heart of a person's problems than through the dream.

Thus the dream is an invaluable counselor. We cannot pay for a better one. It is with us every night and charges no fee except that we listen to it and learn to receive its instructions and heed its warnings. It seeks to cooperate with God's great purpose to bring man to full realization of every part of his potential. It helps to bring him into harmony with himself and God and the world around him.

The Quest Goes On

Lillie and I have settled in Melbourne, Florida, which serves as our base for a teaching and writing ministry. I teach local Bible classes and speak to groups, and we continue to conduct seminars wherever the Lord calls, in the United Sates and abroad. To date, our ministry has taken us to about 40 countries.

Our primary focus continues to be on how God can guide us through dreams and other means. Our knowledge of dream interpretation has never stopped growing, and we continue to make new discoveries about ourselves, for the understanding of dreams, like the understanding of ourselves, is a lifetime process. When I get discouraged, however, I usually have a dream like the one I had just recently:

I dreamed I was speaking German and garlic and Italian, and another language I did not remember.

Though I knew the dream was speaking a symbolic language, it surprised and rather amused me that *garlic* was included as a language. So I stopped to listen to what the Lord might be saying to me.

Speaking in German, I concluded, meant I was speaking honestly, but perhaps a bit forthrightly and bluntly as the typical

German often does. Speaking Italian meant that my emotions were involved. But how could I speak *garlic?*

On one hand, garlic produces a pungent breath that offends people. On the other, garlic is a good food with medicinal properties. It is both offensive and medicinal.

Then I considered the setting of the dream. I had just had the difficult task of telling an unpleasant truth to someone. In the process, I had been frank and honest, and also emotional. How else should I have handled the offensive part, since I knew the truth would eventually bring healing?

Searching the Scriptures, I read what Paul wrote in II Corinthians 2:14, 15: "Christ . . . manifests through us the sweet aroma of the knowledge of Him in every place. For we are a fragrance of Christ to God among those who are being saved and among those who are perishing." The Scripture seemed to say that we are always to be pleasant to everyone. However, in the next verse (v. 16), Paul went on to say, "To the one an aroma from death to death, to the other an aroma from life to life." Out of these I have formed the following prayer:

"May I be a fragrance of Christ to God, of life to that which needs to live, and of death to that which needs to die. May I speak the truth in love and let my emotions be ruled by the Holy Spirit. And may the fragrance of Christ be always upon me."

How revealing that one-sentence dream has been to me! I have come a long way from the insecure person who was too eager to please others, who was often reluctant to take aggressive leadership.

How grateful I am that I heeded the warning of the dream I described at the beginning of this book, because it led me to the kind of exciting, adventuresome life I might never have found otherwise. And I'm so thankful for my wife, Lillie, whose love, honesty, and devotion to the Lord has helped me to change and grow over these last fifteen years. They have been such fulfilling years—because we have let the Lord be in control of our lives.

Index

CHRISTIAN HERALD ASSOCIATION AND ITS MINISTRIES

CHRISTIAN HERALD ASSOCIATION, founded in 1878, publishes The Christian Herald Magazine, one of the leading interdenominational religious monthlies in America. Through its wide circulation, it brings inspiring articles and the latest news of religious developments to many families. From the magazine's pages came the initiative for CHRISTIAN HERALD CHILDREN'S HOME and THE BOWERY MISSION, two individually supported not-for-profit corporations.

CHRISTIAN HERALD CHILDREN'S HOME, established in 1894, is the name for a unique and dynamic ministry to disadvantaged children, offering hope and opportunities which would not otherwise be available for reasons of poverty and neglect. The goal is to develop each child's potential and to demonstrate Christian compassion and understanding to children in need.

Mont Lawn is a permanent camp located in Bushkill, Pennsylvania. It is the focal point of a ministry which provides a healthful "vacation with a purpose" to children who without it would be confined to the streets of the city. Up to 1000 children between the ages of 7 and 11 come to Mont Lawn each year.

Christian Herald Children's Home maintains year-round contact with children by means of an *In-City Youth Ministry*. Central to its philosophy is the belief that only through sustained relationships and demonstrated concern can individual lives be truly enriched. Special emphasis is on individual guidance, spiritual and family counseling and tutoring. This follow-up ministry to inner-city children culminates for many in financial assistance toward higher education and career counseling.

THE BOWERY MISSION, located at 227 Bowery, New York City, has since 1879 been reaching out to the lost men on the Bowery, offering them what could be their last chance to rebuild their lives. Every man is fed, clothed and ministered to. Countless numbers have entered the 90-day residential rehabilitation program at the Bowery Mission. A concentrated ministry of counseling, medical care, nutrition therapy, Bible study and Gospel services awakens a man to spiritual renewal within himself.

These ministries are supported solely by the voluntary contributions of individuals and by legacies and bequests. Contributions are tax deductible. Checks should be made out either to CHRISTIAN HERALD CHILDREN'S HOME or to THE BOWERY MISSION.

Administrative Office: 40 Overlook Drive, Chappaqua, New York 10514
Telephone: (914) 769-9000